LEAVES: their amazing lives and strange behavior

LEAVES:
their amazing lives

HOLT,
RINEHART
AND WINSTON

and strange behavior

JAMES POLING

NEW YORK · CHICAGO · SAN FRANCISCO

Books for Young People by James Poling

LEAVES: their amazing lives and strange behavior

THE STORY OF TOOLS: How They Built Our World and
Shaped Man's Life

THE MAN WHO SAVED ROBINSON CRUSOE

ANIMALS IN DISGUISE

ALL BATTLE STATIONS MANNED: The U. S. Navy
in World War II

contents

Contents

LEAVES: their amazing lives and strange behavior

1: all flesh
is grass

LEAVES BLANKET the earth. Leaf-bearing plants grow in the depths of the sea as well as in desert sands. More than 700 species grow above the Arctic Circle, including miniature trees no more than two inches high that are sometimes overshadowed by the leaves of grass surrounding them. There are plants that grow through the permanent snow on high mountain peaks. The sky-pilot plant has been found within six feet of the 14,495-foot summit of Mount Whitney in California. There is even a buttercup that can bud in the depths of a snow bank. Indeed, about the only places leaf-bearing plants are never found are on the sides of active volcanoes and on the polar icecaps.

Because they are so commonplace, most of us tend to take leaves for granted and pass them by without giving them a thought. Yet every leaf you see is busily engaged in the world's most important single manufacturing process. For while leaves on an average are no thicker than this printed page, they are all in a very real sense highly complex chemical factories. Moreover, the machinery housed within their paper-thin structures is unbelievably more productive than any man has yet invented. It is machinery that makes use of raw materials drawn from the air, from the soil, and from water. And it runs on energy provided by the sun's rays, which plunge into leaves at an astronomical speed that bridges the 93-million-mile gap between the sun and the earth in eight minutes.

In terms of tonnage, the output of the earth's immense foliage factory makes man's industrial production seem puny. For example, in an average year, when the world's steel mills are turning out 500 million tons of steel and its cement factories 350 million tons of cement, the world's green plants are turning out 200 *billion* tons of material.

But it is what leaves manufacture, not its tonnage, that is important, for it is nothing less than the basic foodstuff of all life, be it the life of a violet, an oak, a spider, an elephant, or a man. It is the foodstuff on which plants thrive and grow and with which they build stems and seeds and flowers and all their other body parts. And it is also the food that gives us our energy and strength and from which we build our flesh and bone. Thus every member of the animal kingdom gets all of its food from the plant world, by one path or another, and as inhabitants of that kingdom, human beings are no exception.

Flesh-eating wild animals, for instance, devour smaller animals that live on vegetable diets. As for us, we of course get vegetables and cereal grains directly from the plant world. And foods like milk, cheese, butter, and steaks also come to us from the plant world, by way of browsing cattle. Even Eskimos who live entirely on a meat diet, as some do, feed on animals and fish that depend on plant life for their food. So for all of us, as

2

well as for all other living creatures, the ancient saying that "All flesh is grass" is unarguably true.

In addition to being the first link in what is called the world's "food chain," leaves also help supply us with the very breath of life. They do this by discharging into the air what is for them a useless by-product of their food-manufacturing process. Fortunately for us, this waste product is oxygen, the life-sustaining element in the air we breathe. It has been estimated that for untold centuries leaves have been discharging about forty billion tons of oxygen a year into our atmosphere. It is believed, too, that if they hadn't made this purifying contribution to our air, all animal life on earth would long ago have flickered out like a candle lowered into a container of carbon dioxide.

Leaves, then, are clearly as necessary to us as they are to the plants on which they grow. For without them we would all starve to death—if we didn't suffocate first. Thus the story of leaves is more than a mere description of one of nature's many remarkable creations. It is in addition the story of the all-important role leaves play in Nature's pageant of life. Once you know what leaves are made of, and how they live their lives, you will find that you and leaves have more in common than you perhaps realize. For flesh and grass are alike in more ways than one.

Curiously enough, the story of leaves begins with a man who ignored them. It never occurred to him that leaves play a major part in Nature's scheme of things. In fact, had anyone told him that he couldn't survive without leaves, he would almost certainly have scoffed at the idea. Yet it was his destruction of a centuries-old belief about plants that led to the discovery that leaves are indeed the chief support of life on earth.

The man who gave the study of plants new direction was a Belgian named Jan Baptista van Helmont, who lived from 1577 to 1644. And the experiment for which he is remembered was born of his doubts about a theory developed by Aristotle. In daring to question Aristotle, Van Helmont in his way was as bold as Columbus had been when he challenged the universal belief of his day that the earth was flat. For while Aristotle was a Greek scholar who lived far back in the third century B.C., he was considered such an outstanding authority on natural history that in Van Helmont's time his word on the subject was still regarded as gospel, although it was even then almost two thousand years old.

But Van Helmont refused to take anything for granted. He believed that to get at the truth of the physical world one had to experiment and make measurements and observations. And because he believed this so strongly, he dared question Aristotle's blunt statement that "plants draw all of their food from the soil in which they are rooted." The theory seemed logical, but Aristotle offered no evidence in support of his claim. And Van Helmont didn't like guesswork. He wanted proof. So he decided to test Aristotle's theory with an experiment which scientists today still praise for "its beautiful simplicity."

Van Helmont planted a five-pound willow-tree seedling in a tub into which he had packed exactly two hundred pounds of soil. Then for five years he patiently watered the willow until it grew into a small tree. Finally, on the fifth anniversary of the willow's life in the tub, he carefully removed the tree and its roots from the soil in which they had grown.

The tree had increased in weight from five pounds to one hundred and sixty-nine pounds and three ounces. Yet the soil, to which nothing but water had been added, still filled the tub to its brim. And when Van Helmont weighed it, he said, "I got

4

the same two hundred pounds I started with, less about two ounces. Therefore, the one hundred and sixty-four pounds of [added] wood, bark, and root arose from water alone!" As an afterthought, he said that he hadn't bothered to "take the weight of the foliage that fell each autumn." He obviously didn't think his willow's leaves were of any importance.

Van Helmont had proved Aristotle wrong. But to a considerable degree, he was wrong too. It's since been said that both men went wrong because "in trying to get at the root of the matter they neglected to look up to the leaf of things." They both thought plants were entirely dependent on their root systems for their food supply. Consequently, Van Helmont's claim that his willow's new growth arose from water *alone* was as mistaken as Aristotle's belief that plants feed only on materials drawn from the soil.

However, the fact that Van Helmont missed the mark in no way lessens the importance of his experiment. For one thing, by destroying the two-thousand-year-old Aristotelian theory it removed a roadblock to men's thinking and stirred up a new interest in the study of plant life. For another, the experiment seemed to prove that water was the sole foodstuff from which plants built their fibrous or wooden bodies. But how could plants possibly make either hard wood or tough fiber out of something as unsubstantial as water?

This was the problem Van Helmont posed for the generations of scientists who followed him. To solve it they had to turn to experiments and laboratory tests and forget the ancient books they'd put their trust in for so long. In other words, they had to follow Van Helmont's example. That is why he is considered the father of the scientific study of plant growth, which still remains the most important field of research in all botany.

The distinction of being the first man to look up to the leaf to get at the root of the problem goes to an amateur botanist who published a prophetic book in 1727, less than a century after Van Helmont's death. He was an English country clergyman, the Reverend Stephen Hales, who turned to the fruit trees in his orchard to see if he could discover what happened to all of the water their roots absorbed.

He found that when he cut into a tree's trunk, water oozed from the wound. The same was true when he cut into a tree's upper limbs. And it was still true when he cut into its topmost leaf-bearing branches. This proved that water didn't undergo any change in a tree's roots. Instead, it flowed through a network of natural pipelines that led from the roots to the trunk, then up the trunk and out along the branches to the leaves, where the pipelines ended.

He also learned that the uphill flow of water to the leaves lasted throughout the entire growing season. Why, then, didn't the water pouring into the leaves, day after day, cause them to swell up like balloons and eventually burst? The Reverend Hales's answer came very close to the truth. As he put it, when leaves get too much water, they "perspire." He came equally close to the truth, too, when he said that the reason water was able to flow uphill in a plant, in total defiance of the law of gravity, was that it was sucked skyward by the "pull of the perspiration" of its leaves.

These were theories the clergyman by his own admission couldn't prove. Nor could he prove the amazingly accurate predictions about the mechanics of leaves made at the end of his book. After first stating his firm belief that more than water was involved in plant growth, he then suggested, "May not sunlight, by freely entering the expanded surfaces of leaves, contribute much to ennobling vegetables?" Following this, he again put his finger on the truth with his final guess that, "Plants very probably draw thro' their leaves some part of their nourishment from the air."

As might be expected, his unproven theories caused a lot of eyebrows to rise in disbelief, and none more so than his suggestion that leaves draw nourishment from the air. To many of his fellow botanists it sounded as if he were saying leaves could breathe. And this was surely too far-fetched an idea to be taken seriously.

It may have seemed far-fetched then, but within fifty years a self-taught English chemist named Joseph Priestley proved to the world that leaves do breathe in their own unique way.

It had long been known that if mice were placed in a sealed jar their breathing so changed the air inside the jar that they soon died of suffocation. But no one then understood the nature of the change, and Priestley had set out to find the answer. In the course of his experiments he put a mint plant inside a jar in which some mice had died, to see if the air that killed them would kill the plant too. He found instead that the plant thrived, and in addition so "restored the health of the injured air" that in short order it was no longer "at all inconvenient to mice."

He repeated the experiment, using different species of plants, and always got the same results. In 1774 Priestley wrote, "I have discovered . . . [that] plants reverse the effects of animal breathing and tend to keep the air sweet and wholesome when it becomes noxious in consequence of animals either living or dying in it."

His curious use of language is understandable. Priestley was writing at a time when the science of chemistry was still so much in its infancy that neither atoms, molecules, nor most of the ninety-odd chemical elements found in nature had yet been identified or named. Consequently, he didn't know that all matter in the world is made up either of elements or of combinations of elements called chemical compounds. So he couldn't describe his findings in terms of an element like oxygen or a compound like carbon dioxide, nor could he use the chemical shorthand we've come to expect. For in his day the capital letters *H, O,* and *C* did not stand for the elements hydrogen, oxygen, and carbon. And there were no formulas like CO_2 and H_2O to indicate, as they do to us, that the union of two atoms of oxygen with one of carbon forms the chemical compound we call carbon dioxide, and that water is a compound made up of two hydrogen atoms joined to one of oxygen.

Today, of course, we know that Priestley's mice suffocated because they used up all of the oxygen in the air in their sealed jars, and were then left with nothing to breathe but the carbon dioxide they themselves were exhaling. When Priestley put plants in the jars, their leaves soon made the air fit to breathe again, because oxygen is the waste product of a leaf's food-manufacturing process. Furthermore, in addition to discharging oxygen, the leaves were also soaking up the carbon dioxide saturating the air in the jars—because carbon dioxide, to use the Reverend Stephen Hales's expression, is the "nourishment" leaves draw from the air. It is one of the raw materials they use in making plant food, and they can get it in only one way—by absorbing it from the atmosphere, in much the same way our lungs absorb oxygen from the air we breathe.

With his experiments Priestley unintentionally fathered a custom that we still follow. In those days hospital rooms were kept tightly closed so that no "harmful" air could get in. But after Priestley demonstrated that "plants restore the health of injured air," patients in sickrooms soon began to find themselves, as patients still do, surrounded by plants and flowers of every description. This custom in turn led a Dutch physician to take the next step in unraveling the mystery of a leaf.

Dr. Jan Ingenhousz was like Van Helmont—he took nothing for granted. So as he watched his patients' rooms fill with plants, he began to wonder if they really did help the ailing. To settle the question, he ran a series of tests to check the accuracy of Priestley's findings, and in 1779 learned that Priestley had overlooked one important thing—leaves give off oxygen *only* when the sun shines on them. Thus, once again the Reverend Hales was proved right: as he had suspected, sunlight did have an "ennobling effect" on leaves.

By now a rough picture of a leaf's manufacturing operation had been drawn. With the help of sunlight, a leaf absorbed carbon dioxide from the air and combined it with water drawn from the ground to make the basic foodstuff of life, giving off left-over oxygen in the process.

But just what was this foodstuff? The question was answered in 1804 by Nicolas Theodore de Saussure, a Swiss chemist who finally managed to analyze the substance leaves produce. It turned out to be a chemical compound called glucose—a form of unrefined sugar which, like all sugars, is a mixture of oxygen, hydrogen, and carbon. Glucose is called a simple sugar to distinguish it from sugars with more complicated formulas, like table sugar, and lactose, the sugar found in milk. But there is nothing simple about the role glucose plays in our lives. Indeed, it is so important to Nature's scheme of things that, as we said earlier, the world's green plants turn out 200 billion tons of it annually, or about 100 times the combined mass of all the goods that man produces in a year.

The importance of glucose is twofold. First, it is the fuel that runs all living machinery and, as such, is always present in the sap of all plants and the blood of all animals. Glucose is the fuel that gives a tree the power and energy to push its crown skyward, and it alone gives a football player the energy needed to run for a touchdown.

Second, glucose contains carbon—and carbon is the key atom in every single molecule of every single bit of living tissue in the world. In other words, carbon is one element we simply cannot do without. Yet for all animals, raw carbon, whether it be in the lowly form of soot or in its purest form, a diamond, is just about the most indigestible thing imaginable. In glucose, though, carbon is present in a digestible form. In fact, the carbon in the sugar that leaves manufacture is basically the only form of carbon we can digest, and the only form of carbon suitable for building living tissue. This is one of the reasons "all flesh is grass," one of the reasons an animal's food chain must be linked to the plant world.

De Saussure's analysis of glucose, however, still left unanswered the puzzling question of *how* a leaf manages to make food out of materials like carbon dioxide and water, which in themselves have absolutely no food value. It not only left the operation of a leaf factory as much a mystery as ever, it also failed to explain how the factory got its power from the sun.

Part of the mystery was cleared up in 1818 by two French chemists, Pierre Pelletier and Joseph Caventou. They boiled some green leaves to soften them, then soaked them in alcohol. After a while the leaves lost their color and the alcohol turned green. When the chemists separated the green matter the leaves had given off from the alcohol, they were left with an oily green substance that gave off a heavy scent of new-mown grass.

Further experiments showed that the oily substance was the long-sought link between a leaf and the sun—the miraculous substance that first harnesses the sun's energy, then uses it to make glucose. The two chemists named their find chlorophyll, from the Greek words for "green leaf."

(Although chlorophyll is concentrated in leaves, traces of it can be found in any part of a plant that is green during its first stages of growth. It is also found in primitive leafless plants, like the algae in the green scum you see floating on ponds. It is found too in tiny aquatic plants called diatoms, which form the chief diet of many fish. Here, however, we are concerned only with the leaf-bearing plants, which include some 250,000 of the 375,000 known species of plants.)

Because chlorophyll is a very complex compound, it took almost a century to decipher its chemical code. At first the problem was ignorance. Scientists still didn't know that in plants they had more to deal with than just carbon dioxide and water. Then, in 1840 a German chemist, Justus von Liebig, learned that water dissolves some of the mineral salts in the soil, and is thus able to carry into a plant's roots small quantities of a dozen or so chemical elements, the most important being sulfur, iron, calcium, potassium, phosphorus, nitrogen, and magnesium.

This was a startling discovery because it revealed that plants and animals have far more in common than anyone had ever imagined. For, as you may know, if a human body weighing 120 pounds, say, is reduced to its chemical elements, it consists of about 78 pounds of oxygen, 22 pounds of carbon, and 12 pounds of hydrogen. And the remaining eight pounds are made up of varying quantities of additional elements, the most important, again, being sulfur, iron, calcium, potassium, phosphorus, nitrogen, and magnesium. In other words, the chemical makeup of plants and animals is almost identical. Or, to put it another way, Nature quite obviously created all living things from one basic formula.

As for those who were trying to decipher chlorophyll's chemical secret, the 1840 discovery gave them some clues they had previously lacked. But even so, it still took another seventy-two years to crack the code. Then, in 1912, through the combined efforts of a number of chemists, a molecule of chlorophyll was found to consist of one lone atom of magnesium linked to 136 atoms of nitrogen, carbon, and oxygen.

Once this was known, chlorophyll was immediately nicknamed "green blood." And with good reason, because if you remove the single magnesium atom from the chlorophyll molecule and replace it with just one atom of iron, what you then get is essentially a molecule of red blood—and further proof that nature's formula for life has a common denominator.

But more to the point, with their new knowledge of chlorophyll, botanists were at last in a position to solve the major mysteries of a leaf factory. At the heart of the mystery lay a production line of sun-powered machines, each one so small that 250,000 of them would fit on the period at the end of this sentence.

2. life in a cell

WHEN YOU LOOK at a leaf from a tree, its outward appearance is so deceptively simple that it is hard to picture it as a fully equipped chemical factory. For with your eyes alone you can see only three of a leaf's many parts—the broad, thin, flat portion called the blade; the slender stalk, or petiole, that connects the blade with its parent twig or branch; and the network of small veins that crisscross the blade.

The veins supply the blade with water containing mineral salts and at the same time carry off the food it manufactures. This two-way flow never leads to a traffic jam, however, because the veins enclose a pair of hollow fibers called vascular bundles. Resembling two rows of pipe, these bundles run side by side from the blade and through the stalk to the parent branch, then continue on down the tree's trunk to its roots.

One set of vascular bundles, known as the xylem tubes, transports water up to the leaf. The second set, the phloem tubes, carries glucose from the leaf to the spreading roots and other growing parts of the tree. Xylem and phloem tubes make up a plant's circulatory system.

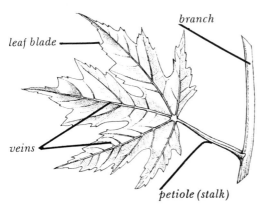

DIAGRAM OF MAPLE LEAF

branch

leaf blade

veins

petiole (stalk)

The stalk, or petiole, does double duty. It is the pipeline linking the blade's veins to the rest of the tree's plumbing system. And it is an arm that not only holds the blade out to the sun but also keeps it fixed in position to make the best use of the sunlight it receives. (Unlike broadleaves, the leaves of grass—corn, oats, and the five thousand other members of the grass family—have no stalks. Nor do the more primitive needle leaves found on pines and other cone-bearing trees. But because they have veins, blades, and chlorophyll, they too manufacture glucose.)

The blade is, of course, the heart of a leaf factory. And while a leaf blade is in itself only about 1/150 of an inch thick (the average thickness of broadleaves in temperate climates), it consists of four even thinner layers of tissue, each of which has its own role to play in the food-making process. Since these layers are too thin for the eye to detect, we have to use a microscope to see their working parts.

When you look at a cross section of a blade through a high-powered microscope, the first thing you notice is that each of its four layers is made up of a mass of tiny objects. These are called cells, and there are an estimated fifty million of them in an average blade. And the fact that the blade is entirely composed of cells is in full accord with the natural order. For just as all non-living matter is a mass of atoms and molecules, every living thing is a mass of cells. For this reason the so-called "cell theory" is as important to biology and the understanding of living matter as the atomic theory is to physics and the study of lifeless matter.

Simply stated, the cell theory holds that:

1. All living things are made up of cells or of materials made by cells.
2. What any living thing is or does is the sum total of the activities of its individual cells.
3. All cells come only from previously existing cells. (In other words, new cells are born only of existing cells, which reproduce by "pinching" themselves in two. And we grow in size only because our cells in a sense multiply by division and increase in number.)

Cells—sometimes called "living building blocks"—are the basic working units in which all life activities take place. Indeed, there are some living things—animals called protozoas and amoebas, plants like algae and diatoms—that consist of but a single cell. In more complex animals and plants, though, you always find an astronomical number of cells. The human body, for example, is a mass of about sixty thousand million cells. And every one of them—be it a nerve, brain, or muscle cell—has a special function.

However, except in cases of single-celled life, cells seldom work alone. Instead they band together to form tissues, which is what we call groups of similar cells that all do the same work.

Muscle and bone, wood and pith, your skin and a potato's skin
—these are typical examples of tissues. When several tissues
unite to perform special tasks, as in the case of a plant's roots
and leaves, they form organs. And since organs are found only
in plants and animals, living things are known as organisms, to
distinguish them from nonliving, or inorganic, things.

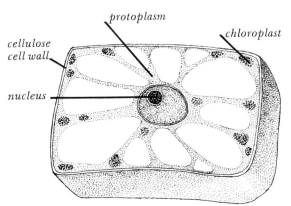

protoplasm

chloroplast

cellulose cell wall

nucleus

DIAGRAM OF A PLANT CELL SHOWING INTERNAL STRUCTURE

All cells are walled in by a
thin, skinlike material called
membrane. The walls, in turn,
enclose a mass of jellylike material known as protoplasm, as well
as a kernel-like part of the protoplasm, called a nucleus. The
membrane in the walls is but one
more example of Nature's incredible engineering genius. For it is
not only designed to allow foods
and minerals dissolved in water
to pass in and out of cells freely. It
is also able to select just those
foodstuffs and mineral salts a cell
needs, while at the same time denying admittance to harmful or
unnecessary materials, much as if it had the ability to taste or
smell!

In addition to having membrane walls, most plant cells are
also boxed in by a second, outer wall of cellulose. Cellulose walls
are meshworks of threads so thin they can be seen only with the
highest-powered microscope. Yet tests have proved that inter-
woven threads of cellulose are stronger than an equal amount of
steel! Equally amazing, plant cells somehow manage to build
their cellulose walls from the most unlikely of raw materials—

the same carbon, hydrogen, and oxygen they use to make glucose sugar.

A cell's kernel-like nucleus is in a sense the foreman in charge of the cell and its cargo of protoplasm, since it alone determines what a cell should do and how it should grow. A nucleus literally inherits its ability to make decisions, because it always receives some of the genes—the units of heredity—that every living thing passes down to its descendants.

Protoplasm is the actual active living substance of life. And we know what its ingredients are, down to the last molecule. But even so, protoplasm is still the most mysterious stuff in the world. For while chemically speaking it is nothing but a blend of completely lifeless elements and compounds, protoplasm is nonetheless very much alive. Why? No one knows. And until we discover (if we ever do) how nonliving matter is transformed into living protoplasm, the greatest mystery of them all—What is life?—will remain unsolved.

As for the chemistry of protoplasm, it was pointed out in the last chapter that Nature used the same elements to create all living things—namely, carbon, hydrogen, oxygen, and nitrogen, and small quantities of a dozen or so mineral salts. These, then, are the elements found in all protoplasm, plant or animal. They are the elemental raw materials with which a cell's protoplasm manufactures, when its nucleus so "orders," the various materials necessary to support life—be they proteins, fats, glucose and other carbohydrates, or lesser known compounds like enzymes, and the hormones which, as we will see later, start and stop the machinery in a leaf.

Yet vital as these substances are, surprisingly enough they account for only 20 percent of the weight of protoplasm. All the rest is water! You may find it hard to believe that 80 percent of a green leaf, as well as four-fifths of your own body, is nothing more than ordinary water. But chemically speaking it is true—and with good reasons.

We already know that water supplies protoplasm with most of its raw materials. But there are two additional reasons for calling water, as one naturalist does, the "very juice of life." For one, we have discovered that the rearranging of atoms and molecules that goes on within a cell's protoplasm can take place only in a watery solution. Water is also a liquid that dissolves all of the vital compounds protoplasm manufactures. Thus it is only by means of tiny streams of water that glucose, proteins, hormones, etc., can move from one part of a living body to another.

So the water that roots absorb and the water we drink is essential to life on three counts. It is the basic broth on which all protoplasm feeds. It is water alone that enables both sap (a watery solution of sugar and dissolved mineral salts) and blood to flow. And water is the only medium in which protoplasm can function.

In one sense protoplasm is the same throughout the living world, because it is always a blend of the same chemicals. But in another sense its mysterious nature is such that there seem to be as many kinds of protoplasm as there are species of plants and animals. This is because different arrangements of atoms in protoplasmic compounds produce different varieties of carbohydrates, proteins, fats, etc. Thus a tree's protoplasm differs from that of a dog.

But the differences go even further. For example, just as the protoplasm in a tree's roots is unlike that found in its leaves, the protoplasm in a dog's brain is not the same as that in his liver. This is why various cells, tissues, and organs work differently and perform different functions.

All of this sounds complicated, and it is. In fact, only those who have spent their lives studying cells really understand them—and sometimes they grow a little confused too.

Knowing how difficult to understand the cell theory is, a famous English scientist, Sir J. Arthur Thomson, once drew a comparison between a tree and a city to help illustrate the role cells play in life. In essence what he said was: Think of the organism we call a tree as a large city. Then compare the tree's organs, like its roots and its leaves, to different sections of the city, such as its industrial quarter and its waterworks. All of the tissues in the tree's organs—such as those in its roots and leaves, and those in the xylem and phloem tubes through which water and sap move—should then be thought of as city streets lined with many small workshops. These workshops are the tree's cells. And inside each shop are shelves stocked with chemical compounds, and a skilled workman (a nucleus) who uses them to make one or more of the many products needed to keep a tree-city running.

It's a helpful comparison. But in order for a city, a workshop, or even a tree to function, it must be provided with some sort of power, or energy. Yet Sir Arthur fails to mention that living cells, like running motors, demand a steady supply of fuel in the form of food. Otherwise they soon stop running and die. And just as diesel locomotives burn oil to get the energy to turn their wheels, cells burn food to get the energy to carry on their work. Moreover, just as diesel engines have fuel lines, plants and animals have circulatory systems that distribute food-for-fuel to their billions of cells.

In living things, the process of burning up food to get energy goes on in all cells at all times. In plants, which use far less energy than you because they move but little, and then slowly, cells burn fuel at such a low rate that their body temperatures are seldom more than a fraction of a degree higher than that of the surrounding air. Because of your much greater activity, on the other hand, your cells have to consume fuel at a much higher rate, which is why your body temperature is 98.6 degrees, even in zero weather.

Obviously, fuel-burning in cells is not a matter of open flames. Instead, it involves a series of complex chemical reactions or changes. But scientists regard these reactions as a form of burning, which they call oxidation, because heat is released when it occurs. Some of the heat that plant cells generate is converted into physical energy, and some of it is converted into more chlorophyll and new vegetable tissues.

It may seem to you that this discussion of the cell theory has taken us far afield from leaves, but nothing could be further from the fact. Because, as it happens, every living cell is dependent on glucose, in two vital ways. For one, glucose is the fuel that cells burn to obtain energy. For another, as was previously pointed out, carbon is the key atom in every single molecule of every single bit of living protoplasm and tissue in the world—and cells can get the carbon they must have to survive only from glucose. In other words, were it not for the chlorophyll we find in green leaves (which makes the manufacture of glucose possible), there would be no cells, no life—and no cell theory.

3: sunlight and green blood

CHLOROPHYLL TRAPS the sun's energy and uses it to make glucose by a process called photosynthesis, which means "putting together with light." Although the process is still far from fully understood, we do know most of its mechanics. Since they are the same in all plants, a look at a single example—a maple tree, for instance—will show us how photosynthesis works throughout the plant kingdom.

At most, an adult maple tree's trunk occupies no more than one square yard of ground. But the tree bears at least 100,000 broadleaves, which give it a total leaf-blade surface of about 2,000 square yards, or half an acre. So the tree has a great deal more leaf-factory floor space exposed to the sun than you might suspect.

While a single leaf manufactures only a tiny fraction of an ounce of glucose per day, work in a leaf factory goes on ceaselessly during every daylight hour. There is no slow-down when the sky is overcast, for even then enough sunlight filters through the clouds to keep the factory running. As a result, it is estimated that in a three-month growing season a square yard of blade surface can turn out a good pound and a half of glucose. With 2,000 square yards of leaves working for it, a single maple tree can thus produce at least 3,000 pounds, or a ton and a half, of foodstuff each summer! (This is why botanists believe that the world's green plants produce a total of about 200 billion tons of glucose a year.)

For the most part, a leaf's manufacturing capabilities lie in its unique chlorophyll-packed machinery. But in part, too, it lies in the remarkable engineering of the four layers of tissue, stacked one atop the other, in a leaf's blade. Because the layers are invisible to our eyes, we again have to rely on a microscope's magnifying eye to see how a leaf factory is laid out, and how its machinery is set up.

Through it you can see how the cells in the uppermost layer have been specially designed to serve as a roof for the leaf. For one thing, they have a coating of wax which makes them almost waterproof. This is important, because water is constantly evaporating from a leaf, much as it does from a wet shirt hung on a clothesline. But with a practically watertight roof, even on very hot days a leaf rarely dries out completely (which could be fatal), though it will grow limp if it loses water at a faster rate than the roots absorb it.

In addition to being waxed, the cells are transparent, to allow sunlight to pass through the roof to the layer of tissue below, where the main work of photosynthesis goes on. As it happens, though, intense sunlight slows down photosynthesis by burning up chlorophyll faster than it can be replaced. Consequently a leaf factory works best at about one-third the intensity of full

22

sunlight. For this reason, plants have had to develop roofs and walls with different degrees of transparency. A maple tree, or any other plant that grows in the shadows of a forest, for example, has leaves with roofs that are almost 100 percent transparent. On the other hand, the roofs of leaves growing in very bright sunlight on an open prairie admit only about 20 percent of the sun's burning rays to their photosynthesizing tissues.

Immediately beneath the roof is a layer of palisade tissue, so called because it is a mass of long, narrow cells which hang from the ceiling in rows that resemble a palisade or a picket fence built of thin stakes set side by side. Most of a leaf's supply of green blood is packed into its palisade cells. And because of this concentration of chlorophyll, the actual production of glucose is of course centered in the palisade tissue.

The palisade cells reach about halfway to the floor, and beneath

SECTION OF LEAF BLADE

cuticle (wax)

palisade layer

xylem

phloem

tracheid (xylem)

sieve tube (phloem)

sponge cell

stoma

them is a layer of plump, irregularly shaped cells jumbled together so loosely that each cell is separated from its neighbor by an air space. Because they soak up most of the water carried to the leaf by the xylem tubes, they are called sponge cells. When the sponge cells are water-soaked, water seeps through their walls into the air spaces surrounding them, where it turns into a thick mist, or water vapor. Then, like a heavy fog, the mist spreads through the blade. And while most of it is eventually

23

lost by evaporation, enough of it remains inside the blade to supply the leaf's other cells with water.

In this way the leaf as a whole gets the water it must have to stay alive. More particularly, the water vapor from the sponge tissue provides the palisade cells with all of the raw materials they need to make glucose. Obviously, the vapor gives them a direct supply of water, but it is also a source of carbon dioxide, since the water vapor dissolves the carbon dioxide a leaf "breathes" in, then carries it to the palisade cells.

The floor beneath the spongy tissue, the underside of the blade, is transparent and waxed, like the roof. In addition, it is also filled with tiny pores called stomata, meaning "little mouths." It is through these small mouths that a leaf takes in air, with its precious cargo of carbon dioxide, and throws out oxygen, the waste product of photosynthesis. These pores are also the openings through which a leaf, as the Reverend Hales put it, "perspires" its excess water vapor. Most stomata are so tiny that 100 would easily fit inside this *O*, and about 100,000 of them serve each square inch of the underside of a maple leaf. (In the grass family, where leaves of course have no roof or floor in the sense a maple leaf does, stomata are about equally divided on both sides of its upright leaf walls.)

Besides looking somewhat like microscopic mouths, stomata also have lips that move. What makes the lips move is an intricate mechanism that somehow enables them to open and close in response to atmospheric conditions. Normally the lips open wide early in the morning. As the day grows hotter, they begin to close, and just before sunset they generally shut tight for the night. On extremely hot, dry days they may open only for a brief time early in the morning, then close for the rest of the day. By closing when the sun is at its scorching worst, the stomata's lips, like the blade's waxed roof and floor, help guard the leaf against excessive evaporation and a possibly fatal loss of water—which is why they are known as guard cells.

To sum up the efficiently designed leaf factory, it has the palisade tissue, with its concentration of chlorophyll, and the spongy tissue that keep a leaf's cells supplied with water. It has a waterproofed and transparent roof, which is filled with pores that control the passage of air and water vapor in and out of a leaf. And it has phloem tubes that carry off glucose as fast as it is manufactured, thereby keeping the leaf factory's production line from becoming clogged.

As for the production line, it is made up of photosynthetic machines called chloroplasts. These are saucer-shaped green disks packed with magic molecules of chlorophyll, and they are almost unbelievably small—so tiny, in fact, that a single palisade cell can hold up to 200 of them. This means that the cells in an area of palisade tissue no larger than a pinhead could contain as many as 400,000 glucose-making machines.

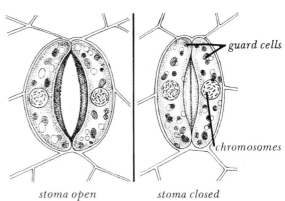

SURFACE VIEW OF STOMA

stoma open   *stoma closed*

guard cells

chromosomes

It would seem from this that chloroplasts might be so tightly jammed together that they are in danger of being crushed. But the subminiature world of the cell is surprisingly spacious. So much so, in fact, that, as one naturalist says, chloroplasts are free to move about "like fish swimming in a pool of protoplasm." Furthermore, their movements are for the most part governed by the burning rays of the sun. When the rays are too strong, they either turn their saucers edge-on to the sun or sink to the bottom of their cellular pool, curl up, and take time out. When the light is just right, they flatten their saucers at right angles to the sun to take full advantage of its rays. And if clouds cover the sun, they all swim to the top of their pool, in order to absorb enough of the sun's waning rays to continue making glucose.

As you know from getting sunburned, the sunlight that affects the movements of the chloroplasts strikes the earth with considerable energy. Indeed, it's been calculated that in three days the sun sends us as much energy as would be produced by burning the earth's entire remaining supply of coal and oil and all of the wood left in its forests. This gives you some idea of the amount of solar energy available to the earth's vast foliage factory. As to the nature of the sun's energy, there is nothing mysterious about it. It consists simply of units of light energy, electron volts called photons (from the Greek word for light, "phos"). In fact, there is no great difference between the photons the sun gives off and those thrown out by a sunlamp, which can also give you a sunburn, or the photons that trace out the picture on your TV screen.

What is mysterious, though, is just *how* chlorophyll traps the sun's electronic energy and puts it to work. For while we know that chlorophyll *does* put glucose together with the aid of photons, or sunlight, we still aren't exactly sure how the green blood of life achieves this miracle.

All we really know is that when the sun's photons strike a chloroplast at the enormous speed of 186,000 miles per second (the speed of light), their energy is somehow captured and redirected by the chlorophyll molecules within the tiny photosynthetic machine. With this converted energy, the chlorophyll in some way manages to split apart the molecules of water (H_2O) and carbon dioxide (CO_2) fed to it by the sponge cells. Next, the chlorophyll rearranges the separated atoms of carbon, hydrogen, and oxygen into tiny packages of solid glucose, throwing off left-over oxygen in the process. To make way for more glucose, the packages are then moved outside the palisade cell, where they quickly dissolve in the water vapor rising from the sponge cells. Once it is in liquid form, the glucose is finally free to flow through the phloem tubes to wherever nourishment is needed in the growing tree.

From photon to packaged glucose, photosynthesis generally takes about thirty seconds. And though in outline the operation sounds both quick and simple, our most skilled chemists have not yet been able to duplicate it. True, they have made a few small grains of glucose in their test tubes—but only after days of labor and with chemicals and extremely high temperatures that would destroy a palisade cell. Yet all during their labors the leaves outside their laboratory windows were of course steadily making glucose, with no apparent effort and at comfortable temperatures.

A comfortable temperature for a leaf, however, isn't necessarily one you would enjoy, because on a clear day a leaf swelters in the same intense sunlight that makes beach and desert sand fiery hot. Consequently, the temperature inside a leaf, like that inside a car standing tightly closed in the sun, may become as much as fifty degrees hotter than the temperature of the outside air. Even so, for a leaf temperatures within this range are not only bearable but also useful, because a certain amount of heat speeds up the chemistry of photosynthesis, just as certain levels of heat are usually required to make new materials in man's chemical factories.

It is possible, though, for a leaf's interior to become so unbearably hot that its photosynthetic machinery will overheat and stop running. However, since leaves are equipped with an extraordinary air-conditioning system, this rarely happens, except in times of drought.

Heat evaporates water, as you know. And water vapor, by dissipating heat in the air, lowers the temperature. Thus as long as water oozes out of its sponge tissue, a leaf is safe. For as heat builds up inside a leaf, it evaporates the water given off from the sponge cells, and the warm vapor that results is expelled into the outer air through the stomata.

In fact, even on mild days, when no air-conditioning is necessary, a maple tree's leaves give off four gallons of water every hour. With a gallon of water weighing eight pounds, this means that the leaves expel twelve *tons* of water a month! What is equally surprising is the scientifically established fact that in a month only one percent—a mere three gallons, or twenty-four pounds—of the tons of water that stream up a maple tree's trunk is needed to keep its leaves alive and working. All the rest is thrown away in the air.

Moreover, what is true for a maple is true for all broadleaved trees and all lesser plants. Indeed, it is estimated that smaller plants commonly throw off half their weight in water every day. And it is further calculated that in temperate countries about as much water is gathered by the roots of plants and then expelled into the air by their leaves as runs down to the sea in rivers!

Why do plants struggle to collect and lift countless billions of tons of water to their leaves and then seemingly waste it? And more particularly, how can a towering tree do what no man can do without the aid of a mechanical pump—force tons of water skyward against the pull of gravity? These questions bring us to the phenomenon of plant transpiration—the word botanists use in place of evaporation, which means the same thing. And we will find that transpiring far more water than its cells need is, in a sense, a plant's way of taking out insurance on its health. We will also find that plants owe most of their ability to suck up rivers of water to the amazing little mouths that dot their leaves.

4: living fountains

TRANSPIRATION WAS FIRST DESCRIBED by that remarkable eighteenth-century clergyman the Reverend Stephen Hales, who wrote of leaves "perspiring" when their roots send them more water than they can hold. Today the word "perspiring" has been replaced by "transpiration," and a definition of transpiration reads: "The normal loss of water vapor by evaporation through the pores (stomata) of a plant's leaves." Both words, however, share the same weakness. Neither of them gives you a sense of the dramatic nature of the process.

To get a better picture of transpiration, think of plants as living fountains, with moisture gushing from the pores in their leaves like fine spray through a nozzle. Since water vapor is invisible, it may not be easy for you to look at a plant and imagine it as a fountain at play. Nonetheless, during its growing season almost every plant transpires enough water to justify the comparison.

It's true of course that a blade of grass gives off only a few drops daily. But each day an acre of meadow grass sprays about six and one-half tons of water into the hot summer air. A much larger plant, such as a growing corn stalk, may expel a gallon of water per day. Thus a one-acre cornfield can transpire 300,000 gallons in the course of a normal growing season—or enough water, if it remained on top of the ground instead of evaporating into the air, to turn the field into a five-foot-deep lake! The most spectacular fountains, naturally, are the trees, with the larger ones, like the great oaks, daily throwing off an incredible 300 gallons, or a monthly total of 36 tons, of water.

Even so, there are times when transpiration can't keep pace with the volume of water flowing into leaves from their roots. This happens when the air is so humid that evaporation almost stops, and when the soil is at the same time soaked with rain. Then water may flow into leaves so fast that they have to fall back on an emergency relief measure called guttation.

EXAMPLE OF GUTTATION

You have probably been fooled by guttation more than once, because on some mornings what you think are dewdrops gleaming on the tips of grass blades and along the edges of other leaves are, instead, droplets escaping from guttation "valves." These are specially designed outlets at the end of a leaf's veins that open only when the water pressure inside a leaf grows too great to be controlled by transpiration. Once they open the pressure falls quickly, because they allow water to flow out of a leaf not as a vapor but in its more concentrated liquid form.

While guttation is a visible phenomenon, you can never see the normal play of the plant world's fountains. But you can sometimes feel the effect their invisible water vapor has on your surroundings. You feel it on those hot days when you gratefully plunge into the refreshing coolness of a woods. You feel it too if you have a large shade tree over your roof, because in addition to shutting off the sun's glare its leaves also spray enough water vapor into the air around your house to make it noticeably cooler. And you can even tell when the fountains begin to dry up. For the slowing down of the leaves' activities at the end of summer is one of the reasons why autumn tends to be a time of brittle dryness and choking dust.

Transpiration also helps keep the world's water supply in circulation. As you may know, the total amount of water in the world never changes—none is ever lost, none ever added. Furthermore, throughout the world there is an average fall of 340 cubic miles of rain each day, or 16 million tons per second. So worldwide there is never a drought. It's just a question of when and where the rains fall. Your reservoirs may be low at the very time India is deluged with rain. When the Atlantic seaboard is drenched, the Pacific coast may be parched.

But in order for any rain at all to fall, the three forms of water we have—that in our lakes, rivers, and seas; the water vapor in the air and the clouds; and the water trapped in the soil and inside plants and leaves—must rotate in an endless cycle. As you would expect, most of our water returns to the atmosphere to form rain clouds by way of evaporation from the open surfaces of lakes, streams, and oceans. In addition, though, countless millions of tons of trapped groundwater are freed each day, lifted from the soil, and returned to circulation by leaf transpiration. In fact, in some places transpiration is even more important than evaporation from open water in determining the amount of rain the land receives.

Although stomata are the main cogs in its machinery, transpiration would not be possible were it not for the linkage between leaves and roots. For it is quite clear that plants couldn't continue to transpire as much as half of their weight in water each day if this loss wasn't being made good by new water sent to them by their roots. Furthermore, all parts of a plant, its leaves included, increase in size daily during its growing season. So each day a plant's rate of transpiration increases too, because as its leaves enlarge, the number of pores through which they expel water vapor also increases.

All of which means that the burden of meeting a growing plant's ever-greater need for water has to be shared by its roots and leaves. The leaves must not only manufacture all of the foodstuff the plant converts into new above-ground growth; they also have to send to the root system enough glucose to enable that system, in its turn, to produce the new roots needed to satisfy the plant's growing thirst. And quenching a plant's thirst calls for an extraordinary degree of cooperation between its roots and leaves, as many studies have shown.

In one famous experiment, a winter-rye plant was grown in a box holding two cubic feet of soil. After four months' growth its roots were washed free of soil, counted, and measured. It was found that in its search for water this one plant had put out 13,800,000 roots that would have extended a distance of 387 miles had they been laid end to end. In other words, the leaves had sent the root system enough foodstuff to enable it to produce new roots at an average rate of three miles a day. This breaks down to a growth rate of sixty-six feet an hour, or more than thirteen inches per minute! What's more, the spreading roots had covered themselves with an additional 6,000 miles of tiny water-absorbing root hairs. To achieve this fantastic growth, the roots had to add an average of 50 miles of hair a day—and root hairs are so small that it takes at least 100 million of them to stretch 50 miles!

It doesn't follow that all plants grow roots at the same rate, since root systems differ from plant to plant. There are trees with larger root systems, and small plants whose roots wouldn't fill a thimble. Even so, the above example gives you some idea of the bustling activity and constant movement that goes on beneath the surface of a seemingly placid meadow as grass grows into cattle fodder, which may eventually become your meat, butter, and milk. More to the point, the example of one plant's restless search for groundwater may help you understand how the plant kingdom as a whole manages to locate and transpire more millions of tons of water than we'll ever be able to count.

And all of it has to be *lifted* from the ground. Moreover, much of it is raised to heights that clearly call for the exertion of a great deal of force—as in the case of giant redwoods that lift water, dead against gravity, to heights of more than 350 feet. Yet no plant is equipped with anything remotely resembling a pump. On the contrary, their parts are all essentially stationary. How, then, do plants, and towering trees in particular, "pump" water from the soil? It's a question that has puzzled botanists for two centuries, and even now they're not sure they have the complete answer.

Any number of unsatisfactory explanations have been offered, including one that some biology textbooks still carry. This is the theory that water rises through the xylem tubes by capillary attraction alone. Capillary attraction is the force that makes oil run up the wicks of old-fashioned oil lamps. The same force makes liquids travel up thin tubes—but only to a point. As a matter of fact, recent tests have shown that in even the thinnest xylem tubes, capillary attraction carries water no higher than five feet. So capillary action can't be the answer.

Another long-held belief was that root pressure forced water upward. Then it was learned that while some roots do build up pressure (just as pressure builds up in tires as air is pumped into them), there are other roots in which this never happens. We still don't know why some roots build up pressure and others don't. But we do know that where root pressure does exist, it never measures more than thirty pounds to the square inch. And this is only about one-tenth of the pressure needed to lift water to the top of the tallest trees. So at best root pressure can account for the rise of water only in some plants some of the time.

Root pressure probably also accounts for stumps "bleeding" when trees are cut down, and for the flow of sap in maple trees in late winter. What is noteworthy, though, is that a maple tree has to be tapped fairly close to the ground. Tap it higher and you get no maple syrup, because root pressure can lift sap only a few feet. Yet in summer water flows up to a maple tree's crown with ease. Why the difference? The answer leads us to the latest theory about what causes water to rise in most plants most of the time. Maples have no leaves in winter. And scientists now believe that transpiring leaves are responsible for the mighty lifting force that tall trees and other plants possess.

If you think of their thousands of stomata as tiny mouths sucking thread-fine columns of water through xylem tubes, like coke through a straw, it will give you a good though not exact idea of how leaves pull water from roots buried deep in the ground.

35

To be more exact, when water is lost by transpiration or used up in photosynthesis, it creates a partial vacuum within a leaf. This in turn exerts a suctionlike pull on a leaf's xylem tubes. Thus, with every drop of water lost, a new drop is pulled into the leaf. And at the same time, the root hairs at the lower end of the xylem tubes draw fresh water from the soil to replace the droplet just fed into the leaf. In this way leaves can pull water from the ground as fast as it is used or lost, provided the soil holds an adequate supply.

Leaves, then, provide the energy for lifting water against the pull of gravity. But the energy would be lost were it not for the nature of water itself. Water molecules tend to stick together. They grip the molecules next to them in much the same way the molecules in a steel wire hold on to each other. Scientists call this cohesion. A drop of water hanging from the end of your finger is an example of cohesion—of innumerable water molecules clinging to each other with a tight grip.

The more tightly water is enclosed, the stronger the cohesion. And, as laboratory tests have proved, when water is enclosed in microscopically thin xylem tubes its molecules hold on to each other with such a powerful grip that it takes a pull of *more* than 3,000 pounds per square inch to separate them! So a water column in a xylem tube is in effect as strong and solid as a rope. And since the "rope" stretches unbroken from leaf to root, a pull on its leaf end is felt down to the farthest root hair, which explains why the suctionlike tug of the stomata draws water into a root as well as a leaf.

It also more than accounts for a tree's ability to conquer gravity, because a pull of 3,000 pounds per square inch could in theory lift a column of water to a height of 6,500 feet. This means that theoretically leaves could lift water more than a mile into the sky—if a tree should ever grow that tall.

Yet the question still remains: Why do plants lift and transpire such enormous amounts of water?

We know, of course, that water is used in the manufacture of glucose. We know that chemicals have to be in a watery solution in order for protoplasm to rearrange their atoms and molecules into the various substances needed to support life. We know too that these substances can travel from one part of a plant to another only by way of the flowing streams in the phloem tubes. And we know that were it not for the air-conditioning effect of transpiration, the photosynthetic machinery in a leaf would sometimes overheat and stop running.

But we also know that a maple may lift 12 tons of water during a month in which its leaves need no more than 24 pounds of it to keep their machinery running. For another example, a great oak can drink 300 gallons of water in a single day—and use only one quart of it. As to the vegetable kingdom in general, it is estimated that the great majority of plants pull from the soil anywhere from 200 to 1,000 times as much water as their cells require.

So, again, why all this collecting, lifting, and throwing away of water? Botanists believe it is a plant's way of obtaining the hard-to-get chemicals its cells need to do their work.

If you think back to the story of life in a cell, you'll remember that the chemicals that protoplasm works with are carbon, hydrogen, oxygen, and nitrogen, plus tiny amounts of a dozen or so mineral salts such as the magnesium chloroplasts use in the manufacture of "green blood." Oxygen, hydrogen, and carbon are of course plentiful. In most cases, too, the soil offers plants an easily obtained supply of nitrogen. But getting the mineral salts they need often presents difficulties.

Chemically speaking, the word "salt" refers to materials *dis-*

solved out of rocks and fragments of soil. And as you can imagine, many mineral salts dissolve very, very slowly. So the groundwater that seeps past stones and soil particles to a plant's roots carries, at best, only microscopic traces of these essential salts. To make matters even more difficult for a plant, some of the chemicals it needs may be quite scarce in the particular soil in which it grows. Thus a plant's greatest supply problem is that of getting all of the mineral salts it requires.

And just as a tropical islander lets the sun evaporate a container of seawater to get his supply of table salt, a plant also has to rely on evaporation to get its salts. But if evaporation is to leave behind all the salts a plant needs, its leaves have to transpire great quantities of water. This, then, is why leaves are living fountains. Transpiration of vastly more water than its cells use is a plant's only insurance that it will get enough mineral salts, and its only guarantee that sooner or later even the scarcest of the chemicals it needs will turn up.

One more feature of transpiration remains to be told. It is responsible for what scientists call turgor. Turgor is easily understood. When a cell is completely filled with water, its walls are under pressure, and it becomes taut and rigid, like an inflated basketball. When through lack of water a cell loses turgor, its walls grow limp and flexible, like the cover of a deflated basketball.

It is turgor, multiplied millions of times in all of the individual cells in a plant's leaves, stalks, and stems, that gives them their rigidity. You have seen this in celery stalks. When they are fresh and crisp, they break. But as they age and lose their turgor, they become so limp that you can bend them almost double.

Turgor is especially important to broadleaves, because, even more than their semi-stiff veins, it supports the flat, expanded surface they have to expose to the sun to get all of the energy they need to keep their leaf factories running at full capacity.

That this is true is easily seen on those hot, dry days when broad-leaves hang in limp folds. They are limp because they have tran-spired water faster than their roots can absorb it. This in turn has so lowered their turgor that they have lost their rigidity.

EXAMPLE OF TURGOR

limp leaf   *turgid leaf*

Here we see the great paradox of transpiration. Leaves have to waste water in order to function properly. But too great a water loss threatens their existence. For this reason, leaves must be able to exercise some sort of control over their rate of transpiration.

The critical times are those that produce excessive evapora-tion—lengthy periods of great heat and low humidity, or drought, or steady dry winds that suck up moisture like blotters. These are the times when leaves are most likely to give off more water than their roots absorb, the times when plants wilt, sicken, and sometimes die. But because they have evolved ways for hoarding water or slowing down transpiration in bad times, most plants manage to survive all but the worst crises.

For all of them, obviously, the simplest way to conserve water would be to close all of their stomata for as long as necessary. However, a plant can't keep its stomata shut for any great length of time because this cuts off the intake of carbon dioxide needed for photosynthesis. And for a growing plant, when photosynthesis ends, starvation begins. So plants have had to develop physical characteristics with which to control their rate of water loss without at the same time bringing photosynthesis to a lengthy halt.

For example, all of the leaves we've discussed up to now—the ordinary broadleaves, needlelike leaves, and grass leaves—characteristically close their pores during the afternoon when the sun is at its scorching worst and keep them closed until the cool of the following morning. And the fact that the stomata of broadleaves are concentrated on their shaded, cooler undersides is clearly not an accident, but part of Nature's plan.

Needles, though they lack a broad underside, also have a special physical characteristic for slowing down their rate of transpiration—a much heavier outer coating of wax than the thin layer which only partially waterproofs the average broadleaf. As for the grass family, with its upright blades, many of its members actually roll their leaves into tubes when water is in scant supply, to reduce the amount of leaf surface exposed to the sun and to drying winds.

However, it would be misleading at the end of the story of transpiration to leave the impression that controlling water loss is a problem for all plants. It *is* true for the vast majority of them, because most plants live on land. But it is untrue for the relatively few water dwellers among the leaf- and flower-bearing plants, since obviously they are never at a loss for water. Indeed, with their leaf factories having the same requirements as those of land plants, they are seldom at a loss for anything. They all grow within reach of the sun, whose rays easily penetrate water to depths of twenty or more feet. And the water they live in contains hydrogen, oxygen, dissolved mineral salts, and a rich solution of carbon dioxide which has been absorbed from the air flowing over the water's surface.

Thus all of the raw materials any leaf factory needs are in water for the taking. And aquatic plants can take them at will, because all of them have developed a special absorbent skin tissue through which liquid-chemical foodstuffs are easily drawn into their bodies. Moreover, some aquatic plants make the best of both worlds. A water lily, for example, has in addition to its absorbent underwater skin a floating leaf that has air-passing stomata on its exposed surface. Plants that grow half in, half out of the water frequently have two sets of leaves—one set, with stomata, for use above water; another set, without stomata, for underwater use. As for those aquatic plants that live completely submerged, not only their leaves but also their entire bodies are equipped to absorb liquid food as fast as it is needed.

With a rich diet always available, it's hardly surprising that water plants usually grow in such profusion that they become a nuisance, clogging waterways, snagging fishing lines, and generally making life miserable for water sportsmen. What is surprising, though, is that these all-too-healthy plants are descended from weaklings. For botanists agree that their ancestors first grew on land, only to be driven into the water by other, more rugged land plants that crowded them out of their original homesites. Their retreat to the water is assumed to have taken a few million years, which in evolutionary terms isn't an unusual time span. But considering that they had to adjust themselves to a totally new environment, today's water dwellers are clearly an outstanding example of a retreat turned into a victory.

They are also an unusual example of what is biologically known as adaptation—an adaptation being any change taking place over the centuries in either the physical structure or the behavior of a plant or animal that makes life easier for it or helps it survive in the face of threatened extinction. And as we will see, in order to win the battle for survival, many plants have had to adapt their leaves in extraordinary ways—some even to the point where they are no longer recognizable as leaves as we know them.

5: how leaves
meet nature's challenges

ALMOST WITHOUT EXCEPTION, adaptations are the product of long centuries of evolution and the ruthless weeding-out process we call the law of natural selection—the law that gave rise to the expression "the survival of the fittest."

The law was first outlined by a great English scientist, Charles Darwin, in a book published in 1859, *The Origin of Species*. In it Darwin explained why all living things have to adapt themselves to the conditions under which they live, or die. It is because life is in a sense an elimination contest in which nature destroys the unfit and selects for survival only those species which are best suited, or adapted, to withstand the hardships and perils of their environment. With his law, Darwin for the first time threw light on many of the dark mysteries of nature that had long puzzled science.

To get an understanding of the role of adaptations in natural selection, you have only to look at the history of the cone-bearing (coniferous) trees, better known to most of us as the evergreens that furnish us our Christmas trees. From their fossil remains we know that the ancestors of today's evergreens first appeared on earth some 200 million years ago. It was in the age of the dinosaur, and at a time when the vast humid swamps that had covered much of the earth's surface for millions of years were just beginning to vanish.

Over the next hundred or so million years, rising mountain chains interfered more and more with the hitherto even distribution of rain. The ground began to harden. Many lakes and ponds disappeared, leaving immense areas of dry sand and rock behind. Changing wind patterns brought cold weather farther south than it had ever before been felt. It was an era of great change in both soil and climate, changes so severe that many species of prehistoric plants and animals were killed off, including the dinosaurs. Yet the evergreens managed to survive. Indeed, they met the formidable challenge of bitter weather, sandy soil, rocky ground, and increasingly dry land surfaces so well that their survival is regarded as one of the great triumphs of plant life on earth.

Not only did the cone-bearers survive conditions that killed off the most gigantic reptiles the world has ever seen; over the long span of geological history the conifers also displayed such an amazing adaptability to a wide variety of environments that they developed 540 different species—each of which at one time or another had to abandon its ancestral growth pattern for one better suited to the particular soil and climate in which it evolved.

Today these species range from the lowly scrub pine to the majestic redwoods and sequoias and include the spruces, firs, cedars, and hemlocks. As forest trees, most of them are so hardy that they reach toward the Arctic Circle, cover great areas of the colder parts of the earth's surface, and climb mountain slopes to heights reached by no other trees. Many also thrive in mild climates, some are at home in semidesert regions, and one at least still clings to life in one of the world's driest deserts. In other words, in terms of the law of natural selection the conifers have proved beyond dispute their fitness to survive.

To a large degree their success can be traced to their needle-like leaves, and the adaptations they have made in them. Needles contain chlorophyll and have stomata just as broadleaves do. But they have an inner content of resin, which flat leaves lack, and a heavier outer coating of wax—a combination that makes them far more weather-resistant than broadleaves. And while conifers do shed, their needles drop off and are replaced a few at a time throughout the year, never all at once. So most conifers are equipped with green leaves the year around, ready to do their work whenever the weather permits. (However, there are two American conifers that can't be called "evergreens," because they drop their leaves in the fall—the larch of our northern woods and the bald cypress in the South.)

A needle's special weatherproofing gives it two advantages over a broadleaf. It helps a needle hold down transpiration in extremely hot periods to the point where a pine, for instance, gives off only one-tenth of the water expelled by a broadleaf tree of the same size. And the same weatherproofing also insulates a needle against freezing in cold weather. This twofold ability of a needle both to conserve water and to resist subzero temperatures explains one of the striking features of the conifers—why so many of them are as well adapted to growth in the sandy soils of the South, where summers are hot and dry, as they are to growth on high mountains, where winters are dry and freezing.

Indeed, because they are so little affected by extremes of weather, conifers are uniquely suited to building a forest wherever there is enough soil, of whatever sort, to cover a root. This trait is well illustrated by the Scotch pine. It thrives in the sandy soil and mild climate of the Middle Atlantic seaboard, and it survives with equal ease in a region in Siberia where winter temperatures drop to fifty or more degrees below zero for weeks on end.

As for the evergreen family's ability to withstand drought conditions that would kill a broadleaf tree, a few years ago botanists were startled to discover that at least two of its members have adapted their needles to serve, when necessary, as substitutes for their roots! That is, when they are starved for water, their needles absorb moisture *from* the air instead of transpiring it *into* the air. The moisture they absorb is then somehow passed down through the tree to nourish its thirsty cells. If the needles absorb more water than is needed, the excess is expelled through the roots into the dry ground.

The discovery of a leaf that could completely reverse the process of transpiration—a phenomenon no one had thought possible—was made during a study of the ponderosa pine. The ponderosa, important for its lumber, ranges from the mesas of Arizona to the northernmost Rocky Mountains. And wherever it grows, it receives less rainfall than any other large commercial tree requires, yet still raises thick trunks to heights of 200 feet—an achievement that had long puzzled botanists.

Now, of course, they know the ponderosa's secret. It isn't wholly dependent on rainfall and melting snow, because, with its astounding leaves, it can draw in the night dew and suck water vapor from low clouds. And it is this reversal of transpiration, this adaptive feature of its needles, that enables the ponderosa to raise its tall trunks, despite droughts or the harsh buffeting of drying winds on frigid mountainsides.

Similar studies have since been made of the Jeffrey pine, a tough evergreen that grows in near-barren soil high on the slopes of California's Sierra Nevada mountains. The studies revealed that over the ages its ten-inch-long needles had also acquired the knack of drawing moisture from the atmosphere. So now we know how these two species of pines have adapted themselves to live in hostile environments. It seems probable, too, that further studies will show that the phenomenon of the rootlike leaf is more widespread than we know, and that it has helped any number of conifers survive the elimination contest we call natural selection.

The phenomenon may in fact account in part for the most extraordinary example of adaptation in the entire coniferous family, a tree that appears to grow sideways! Bearing a name as fantastic as its appearance—*Welwitschia bainesii*—this rare tree grows in the Mossâmedes Desert, near the seacoast of southwestern Africa. Like other trees, the Welwitschia begins with a small round trunk that grows upward—but only to a height of about twelve inches. Meanwhile, it puts out its first pair of leaves, which thicken and droop to the ground, giving the *impression* that the tree is creeping along the desert floor. It continues to spread for an estimated thousand or more years, putting out additional leaves and slowly increasing in size until it measures as much as fourteen feet around—at which point, one naturalist says, "It looks like a circular table rising a foot above the desert floor."

Once it matures, the tree each year puts out small branches, only a few inches long, from the base of its leaves. The branches then bear cones which would look at home on any pine tree. As for the tree's leaves, they are as grotesque as its stubby trunk.

Instead of producing millions of needles like most cone-bearers, the Welwitschia puts out a mere dozen or so pennant-shaped broadleaves, usually about six feet long and half as wide at their base. Nor is their base the branch from which leaves customarily grow. Instead, the leaves grow out of the rim of the tree's trunk, then droop down until they come to rest on the desert floor—with the result that an old tree looks as if it were wearing a grass skirt.

These weird leaves are linked to a huge taproot that is specially adapted for desert survival, plunging deep into the sandy soil, well below the sand's sun-baked upper crust. It is a mass of thick spongy tissue designed to soak up any rain that seeps through to it, store the precious water, then dole it out, little by little, to the leaves.

In turn, the leaves have very few stomata, all located on their shaded undersides. As a further protection against wasteful transpiration, the leaves have a resinous topside coating that deflects the sun's rays from the cells inside the leaves. With its water-storing taproot and its insulated leaves, the Welwitschia thus has two features common among plants that have adapted themselves to desert life.

But it must have something more. Because while the Mossâmedes Desert usually gets about three scant inches of rainfall a year, there have been periods when ten years have passed without a drop falling. And even the most absorbent taproot can hardly be expected to store enough water to maintain a tree's life for a decade.

How, then, does the Welwitschia survive for hundreds of years under seemingly impossible conditions? The answer seems to lie in its strange leaves and in the desert's nearness to the ocean. For like several other deserts that lie close to a seacoast, the Mossâmedes is frequently blanketed by heavy fogs. And botanists think that in some as yet unknown way the Welwitschia has adapted its leaves to make use of the moisture of the fogs that so often bathe them. They also believe that it is largely because of this suspected adaptation that this most incredible of all trees is able to cling to life under the worst possible circumstances.

What produces such an adaptation? How does a leaf change its ways? It is through what is called a mutation, a word derived from the Latin word *mutare,* to change.

As you know, most of us look like our parents because we have inherited their features, just as they inherited their parents' features. But you know too that a red-haired or a colorblind child, say, is sometimes born into a family with no history of red hair or colorblindness. This is the result of a mutation— an unexplainable change in the pattern of inheritance, a mysterious departure from the normal.

Mutations occur because something—no one is quite sure what—takes place in the genes, or units of inheritance, our parents pass on to us. There are various theories as to the cause, none of them as yet proven. Some scientists, for instance, argue that changes occur when a few of the atoms in a gene get out of place. Others believe mutations are caused by the action of natural radiation on genes.

We know that manmade radiations can cause mutations. Scientists have bombarded plants with X, gamma, ultraviolet, and other laboratory-produced rays, then planted their seeds and harvested an unbelievably weird crop of offspring. Even so, we still have no proof that natural radiations cause mutations. We know only that mutations occur frequently in all living things. And that once a mutation introduces a change in any one member of a species, that individual will pass the change on to its offspring. So it is possible for a mutation in a single plant to lead, in time, to a new strain within a species, or even to an entirely new species that bears little if any resemblance to its ancestors.

Grotesque mutations like those which make Welwitschia scarcely recognizable as a tree are, however, the exception. Most are insignificant, seldom involving more, say, than the color of a flower, or the number of its petals, or the mere shape of a leaf. Such minor mutations have no practical value. But as Darwin pointed out and as we have seen, a major mutation that helps a plant adapt itself to a hostile environment can make the difference between life and death.

This is true of the mutation that produced a leaf capable of reverse transpiration. It is true of the mutations that gave rise to clovers that fold their leaves along the midrib and to grasses that roll their leaves into tubes. It is true of any mutation that helps an ordinary leaf continue to function as a food-maker in the face of conditions that threaten its existence.

And it is equally true of a group of extraordinary leaves. They are all leaves that have taken over some special function in place of, or in addition to, photosynthesis. Most have undergone a physical change to suit them for their new role. And if by chance mutant genes have so altered their appearance that they no longer look much like ordinary leaves, no matter. To botanists, they are still leaves, each with its own odd specialty, each working in its own curious way to ensure the survival of the plant that bears it.

6: from monkey tails to flytraps

IF YOU HAVE EVER SEEN sweetpeas, or garden peas growing, you know they will climb any support offered them. You know that they do their climbing with shoots that corkscrew around a trellis, a grape arbor, or a garden stake like, it's been said, "a monkey's tail twists around a branch." These monkey-tail shoots, which are used by a variety of plants, are actually leaves performing a special function.

Technically known as tendrils, they are leaves that have discarded their broad blades while keeping and extending their stalks, or petioles. Their evolution into monkey tails was prompted by a need to play a special role in their parent plant's struggle for survival—the role of lifting the plant skyward, to bring its photosynthesizing leaves out of the shade and into the sunlight. Tendrils, then, are prime examples of specialized leaves that are completely unleaflike in appearance.

Yet as we have seen, a leaf doesn't have to change in looks to take on a new or additional role in life. The leaves of both the European wormwood and the American brittlewood shrub, for example, are quite ordinary-looking. They also photosynthesize in a normal way. In both cases, though, they are in addition leaves that secrete poisons which the rains wash off onto the ground. This makes the soil beneath them so toxic that nothing else can grow in it. Thus they are leaves that specialize in driving away plants that would otherwise soak up the groundwater their parent plants need.

leaf tendril

GARDEN PEA

There are many more plants that have normal-looking yet poisonous leaves, but generally they produce toxins for a different reason—to make themselves inedible to animals that live on vegetable diets and can injure or kill a plant by stripping it of its only source of food. Consequently, *any* leaf that discourages browsing animals has an added value for a plant.

Leaves that look ordinary enough from a distance often turn out, on close examination, to be blanketed with hairs. In the desert you can find leaves with white hairs that deflect the sun's rays as effectively as aluminum roof paint. At the other extreme, the leaves of Switzerland's famed mountain edelweiss are fuzzy with dark hairs that trap the sun's heat. The sharp, hairy tufts on the leaves of the mullein shrub play yet another role. They quickly and painfully work their way into the lining of the mouth of any creature that bites into them.

Probably you have either seen or heard of Spanish moss,

which is neither Spanish nor a moss but a plant that manages to live on tree branches without roots, thanks to the unique hairs covering its leaves. When it rains, the hairs stand erect and do the work normally done by root hairs. They absorb the rainwater that flows down over them from dead tree branches overhead. And because this water is rich in mineral salts picked up from dead insects lodged in bark crevices and from decaying tree cells, the hairs alone are able to supply their leaves with all of the raw materials needed for photosynthesis. Since the hairs have one thin-skinned water-absorbing side and one thick-skinned nontranspiring side, they can also help a leaf conserve water. When the air becomes too dry, they simply bend down and flatten out on a leaf's surface, with their thick side uppermost. In a sense, they put a lid over the water within the leaf.

The most infamous of the hair-bearing leaves is worn by the stinging nettle, which you may have had the misfortune to encounter. If so, be thankful you didn't brush against the devil's-leaf nettle of the East Indies, because its hairs inject a venom that can cause pain for as long as a year.

To say the nettle is a plant with a hypodermic needle is no flight of fancy. For one thing, its bristles are hollow, with brittle, sealed tips. For another, at the base of each hollow hair is a bulb filled with poison, which rests in a socket in the same way an egg rests in an old-fashioned eggcup. Almost any pressure will break off a hair's brittle tip and drive the needle into the skin. And the same pressure pushes the bulb down against its socket. This forces venom through the tip of the needle in exactly the same way pressure on the plunger of a hypodermic syringe squeezes fluid through its needle.

When you brush against a nettle, hundreds of poison-filled hypodermics go into action. If you're lucky, the burning pain of their injections will go away in a matter of hours. If not, you may need a doctor. In either case, you'll agree with the naturalist who damns the nettle as "the absolute limit in pure, vegetable cussedness."

While only the nettle protects itself with hypodermic needles, numerous plants have in self-defense evolved skin-pricking leaves. The prickles on the edges of holly and thistle leaves, for instance, are hardened extensions of the leaves' veins. The thorns on the common barberry, on the other hand, were once the midribs of ordinary leaves. If you examine a barberry shoot you can actually see how its leaves evolve. At its base you will find normal leaves. Midway up the shoot's "evolutionary ladder" you will see organs—half leaves, half thorns—caught in the act of changing. At the top you will find nothing left but midribs that have hardened into thorns. In moderate climates, however, comparatively few plants arm themselves. And when they do, for some unknown reason their barbs, thorns, and needles are more likely to be modified versions of their stems or branches rather than their leaves.

In the harsh desert, things are different. There more than half of all species of succulents, trees, and shrubs have armed themselves against attack. And in many instances their weapons are specialized leaves. This holds true for grasses with saw-toothed edges, the Joshua tree's dagger leaves, the "Spanish bayonet" leaves of the yucca, the century plant's spear-tipped leaves, as well as many other plants whose leaves have cutting edges. And it is of course especially true of the best-known American members of the succulent family, the desert pincushions we call cacti—from the Greek word *kaktos,* meaning "prickly plant."

You may think cacti are leafless, because over the course of evolutionary history they somehow managed to transfer all their photosynthetic machinery and stomata from their leaves to

GIANT REDWOODS: Some giant redwoods lift water more than 350 feet, dead against gravity. *Joe Munroe, Photo Researchers, Inc.*

PONDEROSA PINE WOODS: Ponderosa pine needles reverse the process of transpiration as their needles draw *in* water from dew and low-lying clouds. *Courtesy of The American Museum of Natural History*

WELWITSCHIA BAINESII: The weird leaves of the Welwitschia bainesii are linked to a huge tap root, specially adapted for desert survival. *Field Museum of Natural History*

POISON IVY: Poison ivy is one of the many plants with normal-looking yet poisonous leaves. *United States Department of Agriculture*

JEFFREY PINE WOODS: The ten-inch-long needles of the Jeffrey pine are another example of natural adaptation to a hostile environment where water is scarce. *Courtesy of The American Museum of Natural History*

SPANISH MOSS ON A LIVE OAK TREE: The leaves of Spanish moss
are covered with tiny hairs which function as root hairs,
supplying raw materials needed for photosynthesis. *Courtesy
of The American Museum of Natural History*

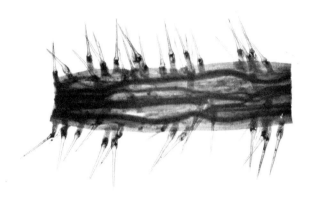

STINGING NETTLES: "The absolute limit in pure vegetable cussedness," the stinging nettle stores its poison at the base of each hollow needle. *Courtesy of The American Museum of Natural History*

CACTUS SPINES: The spiny midrib is all that remains of cacti leaves; evolution has transferred all the photosynthetic machinery to the thick, spongy stems. *Courtesy of The American Museum of Natural History*

Top right, PITCHER PLANTS: Ranging in size from thimbles to gallon pots, pitcher plant leaves grow together to form water-catching containers. *United States Department of Agriculture*

Above, LITHOPS LEAVES: The specialized leaves of the South African lithops protect it from browsing animals. *Russ Kinne, Photo Researchers, Inc.*

Bottom right, SUNDEW: The glue-tipped tentacles of the sundew capture insects, then pull them slowly into the center of the leaf where they are digested. *Courtesy of The American Museum of Natural History*

Above, PHOTOTROPIC MOVEMENT: Light-stimulated auxin causes phototropic movement, forcing the plant to grow toward light. *Russ Kinne, Photo Researchers, Inc.*

Right, VENUS FLYTRAP: One of the most awesome examples of specialization, the leaves of the Venus flytrap are hinged at the midrib and can close like a steel trap. *Courtesy of The American Museum of Natural History*

MULLEIN: These leaves often took the place of a medicine chest in frontier times. *Doug Fulton, Photo Researchers, Inc.*

SEA GRAPE: Sea grape leaves were used as writing paper by early American settlers. *Russ Kinne Photo Researchers, Inc.*

WEAVING ANTS BUILDING LEAF NEST: The ants may construct an entire nest from one leaf. *M. W. F. Tweedie, Photo Researchers, Inc.*

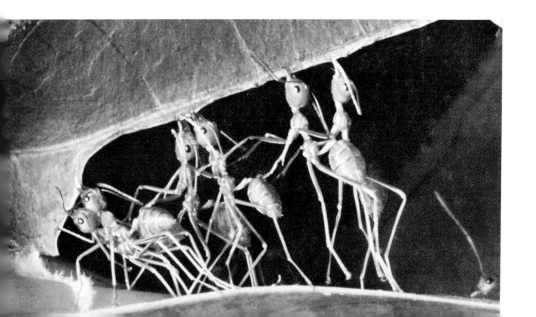

SENSITIVE PLANT: Turgor movement causes the leaves of the sensitive plant to close tightly as the leaflet cells lose water. *Russ Kinne, Photo Researchers, Inc.*

MIMOSA LEAVES: The leaves open by turgor movement as water swells the leaflet cells. *Russ Kinne, Photo Researchers, Inc.*

MAPLE LEAVES: Phototropism causes each leaf on this maple twig to change position in order to receive as much sunlight as possible. *Courtesy of The American Museum of Natural History*

ROSE LEAVES: Neatly snipped by leaf-cutter bees, these leaves have provided building material for the bees' nests. *United States Department of Agriculture*

WINTER BUDS OF THE HORSE
CHESTNUT TREE: These buds,
like other perennials, will
open in response to a
complex natural signal.
*Courtesy of The American
Museum of Natural History*

HICKORY BUDS: These hickory buds have exploded into miniature leaves and twigs on the same day as all other hickories in the area. *Courtesy of The American Museum of Natural History*

their thick, spongy stems, where they store their water. But in the change-over they didn't entirely discard their foliage. Rather, they retained the midribs of their leaves and made of them the barbed-wire entanglement of spines for which the cacti are famous. And in desert regions, where plants can ill afford to have browsing animals destroy foliage or tissues which in moist climates are more easily regrown, the cacti's barbed wire is a pointed reminder to their enemies that they are best left untouched.

But of the many curious desert-bred leaves, the strangest by far are those of the eighty-odd species of lithops native to South Africa. These weird plants were discovered in 1811 by a British explorer, William Burchell, who wrote of his first encounter with them, "On picking up from the stony ground what was supposed to be a pebble, it proved to be a plant . . . [which] in color and appearance bore the closest resemblance to the stones between which it was growing." This is, of course, the clue to the specialized role of the lithops' leaves. Had they not succeeded in camouflaging themselves as stones with the help of mutant genes, they would probably have been browsed into extinction by the hungry animals that roam southern Africa's dry and rocky landscapes.

Most species of lithops consist primarily of two large thick leaves that grow close together in the shape of a cone. The cone's point is buried in the ground and attached to the plant's root system. Only an inch or so of the cone's broad base shows above ground. This is the section that masquerades as a stone; and depending on the species and where it grows, it looks like a piece of weathered limestone, a white-quartz pebble, a fragment of broken slate, even a chunk of iron ore!

But how can leaves possibly photosynthesize when they are

almost completely buried in the ground, away from the sun? The lithops have solved their predicament in a very simple way. The exposed surface of each leaf is dotted with what might be called tiny portholes—small areas of transparent tissue through which sunlight can pass with ease, to fall on the chloroplasts that line the inner walls of the sunken leaves.

A subgroup of lithops has evolved even further in this direction. Known as "window plants," one authority says of them, "They grow with nothing but a flat transparent portion of each leaf being visible, and even that is often more or less covered with sand. Through this 'window,' which is sometimes colored to match its background, the buried section of the leaf receives its light. . . . Nothing appears on the surface except these windows. They peep out of the sand like the eyes of the sand lizard or the sand viper, which often hide themselves in a similar way."

The desert has, of course, no monopoly on fantastic leaves. They exist in every climate. The dense canopy of the tropical rain forest, for example, is due in part to the fact that the forest's thick ground vegetation has forced a variety of plants to take to the trees in order to find a place in the sun. Among the sun-seekers are many relatives of Spanish moss. Like it, they are plants that sprout from windblown or bird-dropped seeds which land in bark crevices high up on their host tree. And while a few of them have developed roots long enough to reach and draw nourishment from the ground below, the rest, with roots fit only for clinging to a tree branch, have to live as best they can.

A few tree dwellers manage to collect their own soil. The nest fern, for one, puts out an overlapping circle of large curved leaves with the shape and function of a basket. Leaves from tree branches above the fern fall into the basket. There they rot and, in time, build up a layer of humus deep enough to cover the leaf hairs that serve the nest fern as roots. (Humus—the layer of dead and decaying plant and animal matter ordinarily found on the surface of the ground—is especially rich in mineral salts.) As nest ferns age and their baskets increase in size, they not infrequently collect a layer of humus so deep that earthworms can live in it quite comfortably. In the jungles of Java, in fact, gigantic two-foot-long worms are sometimes found in humus nests.

The majority of sun-seekers, however, collect water rather than humus. In most cases, too, they are the "pitcher plants"— several families of plants so adaptable that they have two branches, one that lives in trees, one that roots itself in the ground. But wherever they dwell, their leaf edges always grow together to form containers for catching and storing liquids, a trait that has earned them their nickname.

Ranging in size from thimbles to gallon pots, the leaves of some species are indeed pitcher-shaped. Others resemble test tubes, bowls, trumpets, cups, even hollow bananas. Furthermore, their oddly shaped leaves are often so colorful that they can easily be mistaken for flowers. Yet they can all photosynthesize. And a goodly number of them can perform still more extraordinary feats.

True, with one exception the simplest tree-dwelling species merely hold their flaring pitcher mouths open to collect rainwater for their rootlike leaf hairs. The exception is a species that produces an array of ordinary leaves as well as a leaf pitcher and which then sends roots into its pitcher to absorb the water its normal leaves require.

Stranger still are the pitcher plants that dwell in the soil. They are among the 450 varieties of plants that so dumbfounded botanists of old that they christened them the *miracula naturae*—"the miracles of nature." Why miracles? Because of the more than 250,000 higher plants, they are the only ones that have turned the tables on the animal kingdom. Throughout the ages, always and everywhere animals have eaten plants. But the *miracula naturae* eat animals! Specifically, they are insectivorous plants—plants that feast on the flesh of insects.

While each of the several varieties of flesh-eaters has its own method of trapping insects, they still have much in common. They are far more numerous and widespread throughout the world than most people realize. Because they live in soil that is lacking in nitrogen, they all have to get their supply of this vital chemical from the flesh of insects—or so it is believed, though in truth many of the mysteries of these plants remain unsolved. They all trap their prey with their leaves. And usually their leaves are decoys, with a flowerlike appearance and scent that fool insects in search of nectar or pollen.

As for "eating" their victims, although they have no true mouths, the insectivorous plants are all equipped for the task. In addition to being traps, their fabulous leaves function almost like an animal's stomach. They secret digestive juices called enzymes—just as your stomach secretes enzymes to help you digest food. With their enzymes the leaves dissolve a captive insect's flesh into a liquid broth that special tissues in the leaves can then absorb. (In discussing cells, you'll recall, we pointed out that protoplasm is somehow able to manufacture all of the complex chemical compounds—including enzymes—necessary to maintain life.)

To capture their prey, the pitcher plants rely first on the flowerlike lure of their pitchers. Once a decoyed insect lands on a yawning pitcher's mouth, however, the different species trap it in different ways. One species has a mouth lined with hundreds of down-curving hairs, all with a wax coating as sleek and slippery as ice. Consequently, any insect that ventures onto one of these hairs gets an unexpected toboggan ride to the bottom of the pitcher. Moreover, it's a one-way trip. Because when the insect tries to crawl out of the pool of enzyme it lands in, it finds the down-curving hairs as pointed and massed together as a porcupine's quills, to block its escape.

Another species is so quick to secrete liquid wax that the moment an insect lands on the rim of its pitcher its feet are immediately coated with the slippery substance. With no foothold, the creature can only slide down to its doom. Yet another wax-slippery species, common in the Carolinas, adds to its enzyme an anesthetic fluid that paralyzes insects. The anesthesia is so effective that a stack of insects five inches deep is sometimes found in the slender tube of this species' pitchers. And doctors report that as an anesthesia it is in some ways a better painkiller than the novocaine used to give relief to suffering human beings!

Many of these plants have a kind of hood, or awning, over the mouths of their pitchers, to keep out rain. With this cunning adaptation they keep their pitchers from overflowing in a heavy downpour and spilling out some of their captives. At least three species also use their hoods to trick insects that might fly upward and out of a trap. They have transparent spots, or windows, in their hoods, and insects seeking to escape instinctively try to fly through them. You can guess the result. When they bang into the windows, they are knocked back down into an enzyme pool below.

Remarkable as the pitcher plants are, they are no more astonishing than the "flypaper plants," so called for an obvious reason. This group of insect-trappers is made up of 100-odd species of sundew plants and a lesser number of butterworts.

The butterworts have long, narrow, pale-green leaves that curl inward to form glue-filled troughs. The glue comes from thousands of tiny glands that dot the upper surface of each leaf, side by side with glands that secrete enzymes. An insect has only to mire its feet on a leaf's flypaper surface to send a butterwort into action. The leaf begins to squeeze more glue and enzyme from its glands, and at the same time it starts rolling its sides slowly inward, not stopping until its prey is completely enveloped. At this point the leaf remains tightly shut for as long as it takes to digest its meal.

The sundews, though smaller than the butterworts, have a more evil quality. They are ground-hugging plants with round leaves seldom larger than a shirt button. Yet each leaf supports a hundred or more tiny tentacles, and each tentacle is tipped with a drop of glue that glistens like dew. For insects, though, it is a deadly dew, because an ant, mosquito, or gnat need touch no more than two or three tentacles to be caught fast, no matter how furiously it struggles.

And once snared, its fate is sealed. For then all the sundew's octopus-like tentacles reach out for the struggling creature, close over it, and pull it slowly down to the center of the leaf. As they move, they pour out additional glue—enough to drown their victim before it is even tightly wrapped within the leaf. Once the trap closes, the leaf remains shut for several days, enacting the role of an animal's stomach. When the creature has been digested, the tentacles relax their grip, fan outward, and return the leaf to its original position—to lie in wait for another victim.

One last amazing thing remains to be said of the sundew. In some unfathomable way it is actually able to tell the difference between what is edible and what isn't! Drop a tiny pebble on a sundew leaf, and its tentacles, after first bending toward it, will turn away from it. But try dropping a sliver of meat, and you will see its tentacles close over it exactly as they would a trapped insect. If nothing else, this astounding ability saves the sundew considerable time and energy. It never wastes any effort on the chance dirt particles and the like which the winds blow onto its tentacles.

The most awesome of all specialized leaves unquestionably belongs to the Venus's-flytrap, which grows only along the Carolina coast. The great naturalist Charles Darwin rightly called it "the most wonderful plant in the world."

The leaf of the Venus's-flytrap is as brilliantly colored as a flower. It also exudes a sweet nectarlike fluid attractive to insects. Yet the full wonder of the leaf, which may reach the size of a half-dollar, lies in its construction, for it has two halves that are hinged along the midrib so they can open and close like the jaws of a steel trap. Like a steel trap, too, the outer edge of each half bears a row of sharp teeth. In addition, three short trigger hairs sprout from the inner surface of each half. And any insect that blunders into them makes a fatal mistake, because once tripped, the trap snaps shut in a split second.

Once shut, the trap gradually pinches tighter and tighter, pressing its prey closer and closer to its digestive glands, in a merciless squeeze that lasts for as long as twelve hours. Thereafter the flytrap remains quietly closed for a week or ten days, slowly reducing its victim to a skeleton. Then the trap's teeth slowly part. The twin jaws gradually open. And the hungry mouth is ready for its second victim. But after the leaf springs its trap the third time, it turns black and dies. It has done its work, and done it well. Because it has not only supplied the plant that bore it with nitrogen, which is notably lacking in the coastal soil of the Carolinas; but in the midst of its strenuous trapping activities it has also been busily manufacturing glucose!

Like the sundew, the flytrap too can distinguish between what is appetizing and what isn't. In one experiment, for example, a flytrap's trigger hairs were sprung by a blade of grass. But instead of snapping shut, the trap closed very slowly, then opened again in twenty-four hours. In a second test, a sliver of glass was dropped on the trigger hairs. This time the trap spent five hours closing. And it took less than a day to reopen, spit out the glass, and reset itself!

Finally, a flytrap seems to be almost indestructible. It can withstand freezing weather, and when fires sweep across its fields, it is among the first plants to reappear in burnt-over areas. And when it is submerged by floodwaters, it goes right on trapping. True, no one claims that it can live underwater indefinitely. But flytraps have emerged from receding floodwaters with their mouths filled with small aquatic insects, made a meal of them, then reset their traps again—just as if nothing unusual had happened.

Small wonder, then, that Darwin thought the Venus's-flytrap the most wonderful of plants. And when we think of the crafty and predatory activities of all of the insect-eaters, as contrasted to the quiet behavior of ordinary plants, we too can understand why in olden days botanists called them *miracula naturae.* Yet quiet as ordinary plants seem, they too are capable of surprising physical activities. And although they may not perform as spectacularly as the flesh-eaters, in their undramatic way ordinary plants often do things that are equally awesome.

7: on the move

EVERYONE THINKS of plants as fixed, stationary objects, anchored in place by their roots. Consequently, almost anyone who is asked to describe the differences between plants and animals will, for one, mention that animals move while plants do not. Yet in their own way, plants and their parts are fully capable of moving under their own power. And of all of a plant's parts, none is capable of a more astonishing variety of movements than its leaves, even though they are firmly anchored to twigs by their stalks, or petioles.

To be sure, they aren't free to move from place to place as animals do. Nevertheless, they can move of their own accord. For example, we know that a leaf's little stomata open and close their lips daily. Some leaves fold or roll their blades together to cut down on transpiration. We've even seen how with the help of its leaves a winter-rye plant can produce new roots at a growth rate of thirteen inches per minute. Movement, it's clear, is as essential a part of a plant's life as of an animal's.

One of the first to make a serious study of plant movements was the great naturalist Charles Darwin, who in 1880 published a book of more than 500 pages on *The Power of Movement in Plants*. Darwin was chiefly interested in the overall growth movements of plants—the way in which their various growing parts move together to produce distinctly different patterns of growth in different species of plants. In short, he knew that an oak didn't get big or a violet remain small by accident, because nature doesn't leave things to chance. So he was convinced that every plant's size, shape, and structure were determined by an internal growth-control mechanism of some sort. But what kind of mechanism?

Darwin never discovered the mechanism's exact nature. But in one series of experiments he did demonstrate that many of the growth movements of a young plant are directed by the tip of its stem, or trunk. In effect, he found a control center that apparently sent instructions to those parts of a plant which came under its supervision.

Although he couldn't explain the secret of stem tips, Darwin considered the controls they exercised so extraordinary that he wrote, "It is hardly an exaggeration to say that the tips . . . having the power of directing the movements of adjoining parts, act like the brains of one of the lower animals." He knew, of course, that plants have no brains. But he couldn't describe his findings in scientific terms. Nor could anyone else until 1926, when a Dutch college student proved that a plant's growth movements and behavior are the result not of thought but of complex chemical controls.

The student, who later became a great authority on plant growth, was Frits Went. In that year he was serving by day in the Dutch Army and working by night in a laboratory at the University of Utrecht to keep up his graduate studies in botany.

At the time, Went was puzzling over the meaning of certain experiments started by several European scientists who were following in Darwin's footsteps. They had all found that when they cut off the stem tips of oat seedlings the plants stopped growing. Yet they had only to set the tiny tips back in place to start the seedlings growing again! This seemed to indicate that a stem tip secreted a substance that controlled a plant's growth. But none of the scientists involved had been able to prove this was the case.

Went thought of an experiment which would show whether or not there really was such a substance. He too beheaded an oat seedling. Then he set the severed tip on a small block of gelatin for several hours. Next he threw the tip away and attached the gelatin to the headless seedling. This was Went's reasoning: *If* the stem tip did secrete a growth substance, the gelatin would soak it up, just as a blotter absorbs ink. And *if* the gelatin became saturated with the growth substance, when the block was attached to the seedling the substance should by rights pass from the gelatin into the plant's tissue and restart its growth.

And so it turned out. At three o'clock on the morning of April 17, 1926—a moment now considered a milestone in botanical history—Went walked into his laboratory and saw to his joy that the seedling had indeed begun to grow again. Thus with a fairly simple experiment a college student succeeded where experts had failed. He proved that a plant manufactures a chemical substance which plays a key role in the control of its growth, movements, and behavior.

But as Dr. Went says, "Identification of this growth substance proved to be a long and tedious task. At first attempts were made to extract it from the tips themselves, but this approach was abandoned when it became apparent that it would take 10 girls working 70 hours a week 70 years to obtain a single gram of the substance. Other approaches finally led to . . . [the identification of a chemical compound] . . . which was named auxin."

In recent years, scientists have found that plants have control centers other than their stem tips, where they manufacture a number of equally complex chemical substances which in one way or another influence the growth movements of roots, flowers, and leaves, as well as both the development and falling of fruits and nuts. With auxin, as a group these compounds are known as growth regulators. As a group, too, they have one particular thing in common—what a famous botanist ruefully describes as "the considerable mystery which still shrouds their actions."

However, since of all the growth regulators Dr. Went's auxin has been most widely studied, we do know something about its actions—including the fact that auxin and leaves are inseparable on several counts. But to understand the curious role auxin plays in the life of a plant and its leaves, we first have to take a look at how a plant grows from a seed to maturity.

Generally speaking, every seed contains a small embryo with a tiny stem, the beginnings of a root, and one or two seedling leaves. Most of a seed's bulk is taken up by its seedling leaves (called cotyledons), which are swollen with stored food. If you soak a lima bean and remove its outer skin, this is easily seen. The two fat halves of the bean, joined like the halves of a clam shell, are the seedling leaves. Between them lies the tiny pale-green embryo shoot and root, ready to draw on the food stored in the fat cotyledons and start growing into a full-fledged bean plant as soon as germination begins.

In the first stage of germination the entire seed swells to the bursting point as each of its countless cells absorbs the water it must have to begin working. Once the cells are active, the embryo can start growing. Pushing up toward the light and down into the soil, its infant stem and root lengthen without thickening. Their growth is made possible by the delivery of a steady supply of glucose to each stem and root cell, from the stored food in the seedling leaves. The more they are fed, the more the cells grow and the more capable they become of absorbing water. And the more water they absorb, the more their turgor increases.

When an ordinary cell is so water-filled that it is in a state of high turgor, you'll recall, its walls come under so much pressure that it becomes taut and rigid, like an inflated basketball. Here, however, we are dealing with extraordinary cells. For in ways too complicated to go into, the cell walls of embryonic roots and stems are built so that they can stretch in only one direction—lengthwise. And under the pressure of turgor they stretch to the point where they can no longer contract, so their lengthwise growth becomes permanent.

This is why a young plant doesn't grow in all directions at once, like a young animal, but only straight up and down. Its growth can be compared to the one-way stretch of a spring as contrasted to the three-way stretch of a balloon. Thus by cell-stretching a tiny embryo begins to grow into a seedling. But for continuing growth new cells are of course needed. And since all

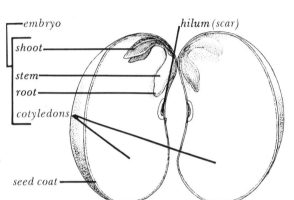

SECTION OF SEED EMBRYO

embryo — shoot — stem — root — cotyledons — hilum (scar) — seed coat

67

growth, plant or animal, comes about because cells multiply in number by dividing, it follows that cell division has to go on constantly in the stem and root tip of a growing plant.

The downward thrust of the lengthening root simply plunges it deeper into the soil. But the upward thrust of the stem carries the cotyledons with it as it breaks ground. Once in the sun, these seedling leaves turn green and continue to feed the stem until its first true leaves appear, at which point they shrivel and drop off.

The most active part of the stem is its tip. It is filled with tiny cells, which are continuously dividing and then increasing in length as much as twenty times, to add to the height of the stem. And while these cells grow largely in one direction, occasionally some of them veer from their path to produce the beginnings of true leaves. But leaf-forming cells never branch out in a disorderly fashion. Rather they form new leaves as if by plan, so that the leaves appear on the growing stem in an astonishingly regular pattern.

The stem displays an equally astonishing regularity in its perpendicular growth. Astonishing, because in order for a stem to grow straight up, its cells all have to grow at *exactly* the same rate. If they didn't, if those on one side grew more rapidly than those on the other, a stem would become lopsided and bent. Yet under normal conditions a stem's growth is almost always rigidly perpendicular. Add the fact that leaves always sprout in a definite pattern to the fact that stems never grow haphazardly and you have clear proof that plants don't grow by chance but are instead guided by one or more growth-control mechanisms.

This brings us back to Dr. Went's auxin. As the growth regulator we know the most about, it is the educated guess of most botanists that auxin probably plays a broader role in controlling the overall growth of plants than any of the other known regulators—but because growth regulators are still so little understood, most scientists would hesitate to swear to it.

Even so, botanists have learned a good deal about the nature of auxin. They know, as Dr. Went demonstrated, that auxin is first produced in tiny quantities in a seedling's stem tip. Later it is also secreted by a seedling's leaves. If the seedling is that of a perennial plant, in future springs when infant leaves and stems burst from their buds, they too will manufacture auxin and continue to do so throughout the plant's growing season. It is also known that the size a plant attains is determined largely by the amount of auxin its leaves and stem tips produce during its lifetime. This is why plants of the same age of any given species are usually about equal in size.

Generally speaking, we know too that auxin molecules move down through the phloem tubes from the stem tips and leaves in which they are created to the roots at the other end. We also think that the first molecules produced in the spring are the biological messengers which, in a sense, spread the word that the moment to start growing has come. Then the cells of roots, twigs, and stalks start to elongate, and an entire plant begins to pulse with life. Thereafter, under the stimulus of a steady flow of auxin, a plant continues its growth movements until the end of its growing season. At this point auxin production stops, bringing growth to a halt. For annuals, this marks the end. For perennials, it signals the approach of their dormant period.

Where broadleaves and their movements are concerned, what we've learned about auxin has removed much of the mystery surrounding the remarkable way in which these leaves twist and turn in response to a phenomenon known as phototropism. (The word "tropism" means "a turning." "Photo" comes from *phos,* the Greek word for "light." Thus "phototropism" means "a turning to light.")

While you may not have recognized them as such, you've seen many instances of phototropism. For one, you've seen how the leaves of a potted plant growing near a window bend toward the outdoor light. And you probably know that if the plant is turned around so that its leaves face away from the window, they will begin to twist and turn and continue moving until they once again face the light.

You may also have noticed another not uncommon example of phototropism. Weed seeds are often blown under the sloping edges of rocks, in a position where sunlight reaches them only at one period of the day, and then only from one angle. When these seeds germinate, finding a place in the sun for their infant leaves is a matter of life itself. Yet the seedlings never engage in the hopeless task of trying to push their leaves through the overhanging stones. Instead, the leaves bend toward the little light available, move out into the open, then turn through an arc of as much as ninety degrees in order to right themselves and reach skyward to the sun.

It's true that leaf movements such as these are as slow and seemingly undramatic as growth itself. However, you have to remember that in addition to being anchored to a twig by its stalk, a leaf has no nervous system to trigger its movements, nor muscles with which to carry them out. In view of all this, you can see that in many ways a leaf's ability to act on its own makes its movements even more astonishing than those of a muscle-powered animal.

How does a leaf execute phototropic movements without the help of muscles? The answer lies in auxin and its surprising reaction to light. If auxin was human, we'd say that it dislikes

70

sunlight and tries its best to keep out of it, though why this should be "still puzzles scientists," according to Dr. Went.

Whatever the explanation, because auxin is light-shy it has a strong tendency to concentrate on the shady side of a leaf's stalk. Thus any stalk leaning away from a light source—as in the case of the leaf stalks of a window plant that has been turned around—receives more auxin on its dark side than its sunny one. And since auxin stimulates growth, the inevitable happens. Influenced by a concentration of auxin, the overstimulated cells on the shaded side of a stalk elongate much more rapidly than the understimulated cells on its sunny side. This lopsided growth bends a stalk back toward the light—and keeps it moving toward the light until the leaf blade the stalk carries with it receives enough sunlight to photosynthesize properly.

Phototropic movement, then, is simply nature's way of guaranteeing a leaf its proper place in the sun. For not only does phototropism literally force a leaf stalk to bend toward the light, it also enables a leaf to change its position on a twig so as to receive as much sunlight as possible. And almost every leaf at one time or another in its life does find it necessary to move in search of more sunlight.

How true this is you can easily see for yourself. Stand under any large tree and look up. The first thing you'll notice is that every available bit of space is filled with leaves, all apparently growing without plan or reason. If you look more closely, though, you'll see that they have grown in a mosaic pattern, and that vast as their number is, they all manage to keep out of each other's way so that there is a minimum of shading of one leaf by another. And the pattern, you'll discover, is brought about to a large degree by the growth movements of the leaf stalks. With auxin's help, at one time or another the leaf stalks have all grown in different ways and directions and to different lengths, in order to bring their own leaf blades into the strongest possible sunlight.

If you examine climbing vines, like ivy, you'll find that they too form a leaf mosaic as they climb a brick wall, with their leaves so spaced that there is very little overlapping. When ivy is used as a ground cover you'll also find that in seeking the sun many stalks made a vertical turn and thereafter grew straight up, because once they became exposed to the sun on all sides, auxin began to flow down each side in equal amounts.

A leaf's ability to change position when other leaves threaten to cut it off from the sun is best seen in bushes that grow in a tangled mass, like forsythia bushes. Separate almost any for-sythia shoot from the others with which it is entangled and you will find leaf stalks growing from it in a surprising number of ways. Some stalks grow from the shoot at a ninety-degree angle, others at no more than a ten-degree angle. Some stalks are straight, others U-shaped, still others C-shaped. Occasional stalks have twisted and turned so much in the struggle to carry their blades into the sunlight that they are practically S-shaped.

Looking at these contortions, it's easy to slip into the mistake of thinking that leaves deliberately and purposely set out in search of the sun. But plants have no purposeful intelligence, no brain to tell them that their survival depends on their moving their leaves into a position where they can get enough of the sun's energy to photosynthesize effectively. All they have is auxin. And that is enough. Because as we have seen, for a leaf auxin is a perfectly satisfactory substitute for a brain—which only adds to the wonder of this strange and mystifying growth substance.

Turning from the phototropic activities common to all broadleaves, we now come to some rarer and even stranger leaf movements. First there is thigmotropism, or moving in response to contact or touch. The power of thigmotropic movement is for the most part limited to tendrils, those specialized leaves which wind around a support like a monkey's tail twists around a branch. Tendrils, you'll recall, are put out by garden and sweet peas, morning glories, and other climbing plants. And some tendrils are so sensitive to contact that they begin coiling around a solid object within a couple of minutes of touching it, even if it is no more substantial than a silk thread! To wind around a garden stake, or any other object, we know that the cells on the side of the tendril away from the stake have to elongate suddenly and much more rapidly than those on the side touching the stake. But exactly what causes the cells to elongate so rapidly is unknown. Thus thigmotropism remains one of nature's secrets.

The "sensitive plant," a species of mimosa, is so named because its compound leaves also move in response to contact or touch. (A compound leaf has a row of small leaflets branching out of each side of its midrib, as in the case of a fern leaf.) What's more, the plant is so sensitive that you can actually tease it. If you touch the expanded leaflets at the tip of one of its leaves, they will immediately fold shut, and then one by one the other leaflets along the midrib will follow suit. In a moment or two all of the leaflets will be closed, and little can be seen except an apparently bare midrib. After several minutes, though, the leaf opens up again. Touch it once more, and it will again collapse. But if you touch the leaf repeatedly, you will find that each time it stays closed for a longer period. The leaf of a sensitive plant seems to find continued teasing as disturbing as we do.

However, the leaf's response to touch is not an example of thigmotropic movement, as you might think. It is an example of what is called turgor movement. In the sensitive plant, cells at the base of its leaflets lose water whenever its leaves are touched or jarred. As they lose water they grow limp and the leaflets droop. In time the cells regain water, and as they stiffen they lift the leaflets back into their normal position. Another example of turgor movement is the rolling up of grass leaves in dry spells, previously mentioned. They roll into tubes because certain cells along their edges lose water more readily than others.

The swelling and shrinking of specialized turgor-powered cells also explains the traplike action of the two halves of the leaves of the Venus's-flytrap. Specialized cells line its leaves' midribs. There they act as hinges, remaining open when they are limp, swinging shut when water pours in to swell and stiffen them.

Any number of plants—beans, laburnum, gorse, pigweed and jewelweed, among others—have leaves that display so-called "sleep movements." In other words, their leaves either droop or close at nightfall, then rise or open again when the sun reappears. Naturally, such movements have nothing to do with sleep. Instead, they are probably connected with the nightly closing of leaf factories and their reopening in the morning. Or, as Dr. Went says, they may be "just another instance of the daylight-darkness rhythm so common in plants."

There is nothing common, however, about the daylight-darkness rhythm of the mallowweed's leaves. For here are leaves that actually move with the sun as it moves through the sky. Moreover, should a tree trunk block the sun from their view, they stop dead in their tracks. But as soon as the sun strikes them again, they hurriedly change position so that they once more face it squarely. And when the sun sets, they do an actual about-face. They immediately begin to turn from west to east to greet a sunrise that is still hours away! Watching this incredible sight tempts one to believe that instead of a built-in rhythm mallow leaves have a built-in intelligence that tells them where the sun will reappear—which, of course, they don't have.

Finally we come to the weirdest of all leaf movements—those of the Asian telegraph plant. This is a plant whose leaves are in constant motion all day long. Sometimes they all move in little circles. Sometimes the leaves on one side of the plant's stem are moving up while those on the opposite side are moving down. And sometimes its leaves seem to run wild, some moving up, some down, some circling—like signal flags spelling out a message that no one has yet been able to read. For as Sir Arthur Thomson says, "No one has the slightest idea why the leaves of this plant should be so continuously busy."

The telegraph plant is a freak of nature, and a mysterious one. But it does send out one readable message. It tells us more emphatically than any other plant that leaves *can* move under their own power, and move in an impressive number and variety of ways.

8. in use

WE NOW KNOW that all flesh is grass, and that because leaves manufacture the basic foodstuff of life they alone stand between us and death by starvation. We know too that as leaves manufacture glucose they discharge oxygen, and thereby help supply us with the very breath of life. We also know that, as living fountains, leaves play a significant part in keeping our water supply in constant circulation. These are the reasons why leaves are said to be as necessary to us as they are to the plants on which they grow.

But besides keeping us alive, it can also be argued that leaves help clothe us, since the glucose they produce is the chief raw material that plants use to build their various body parts. Thus cotton is in a large measure an indirect by-product of a leaf factory. So too is linen, which is made of fibers from the stem of the flax plant. As for silk, it's true that it is spun by silkworms—but only by silkworms that feed on nothing but mulberry leaves.

By the same reasoning, leaves play an important role in housing us, because here again they provide the raw materials for the tree trunks that supply us with building timber. In the tropics, moreover, the palm leaf itself is used to shingle millions of native homes. As shingles, palm leaves last longer than zinc roofing in equatorial climates. And since they are waterproof, even in the heaviest tropical rain you can stay snug and dry under a properly thatched palm-leaf roof.

Leaves are also of some medical importance. For example, atropine, a drug used by eye doctors, comes from the leaves of the belladonna plant. Digitalis, a drug used to treat heart patients, is obtained from the leaves of the foxglove. And as anyone who has been nagged into eating spinach knows, some leaves are especially rich in vitamins.

Tea leaves give us one of the world's most popular drinks. Henna leaves yield a hair dye. Leaves of such plants as wintergreen, spearmint, peppermint, sage, thyme, and many others are used for flavoring. Many of our baskets are woven from a leaf tissue called raffia. Palm-leaf fronds are also woven into baskets, as well as into hats and doormats. The wax that covers the leaves of Brazil's carnauba tree is sometimes used to give a high protective polish to waxed floors and automobiles. At sea, rope woven from shredded palmetto leaves is treasured because it is almost rot-proof. The tannin used in curing leather is found in oak leaves. So too are many of the dyes used to color fabrics. Nor does this exhaust the list of commercial uses now made of leaves. But of even greater interest are some of the odd uses made of leaves in the past.

Take, for instance, the romantic history of just one of the several plants whose leaves were thought by our forefathers to have almost magical healing qualities—the mullein, a three- to four-foot shrub with coarse woolly leaves. Today we consider mullein an annoying and useless weed that clings stubbornly to any soil in which it takes root. Yet its past is as colorful as some of its nonscientific names—hedge torch, beardtongue, Indian's paintbrush, velvet leaf, Adam's flannel. Two thousand years ago ancient Greeks banqueted in the light of lamps equipped with mullein-leaf wicks. Later, Roman funeral processions were lighted by torches made from mullein stems and leaves dipped in wax. Still later, in the Middle Ages, mullein tea was for a long time a popular remedy for lung diseases in both men and cattle.

With the discovery of America, colonists with unbounded faith in the mullein's medicinal magic carried the plant to our shores, where it has since spread across the land. On the frontier, mullein leaves all but took the place of a medicine chest. Mullein-leaf broth was used both as a cathartic and as a cure for catarrh. The thick gray-green leaves served as a substitute for scarce flannel in binding up sore throats, and were also substituted for mustard plasters.

If you were a frontiersman with asthma, you smoked mullein leaves to gain relief. If you had rheumatism, you treated it with a mullein-leaf salve. And if you were a true believer, you insisted that juice squeezed from mullein leaves would cure deafness, given enough time. Then advancing civilization brought doctors and drugstores to what was once the frontier, and the mullein was soon forgotten—except in New England, where at the turn of this century farmers were still lining their shoes with a cushion of mullein leaves, to avoid blisters.

In searching through old documents, historians have discovered that leaves were employed in a wide variety of additional ways in our country's early days. For one thing, the record shows that the first Americans—the Indians—were by no means limited to the mere ceremonial use of tobacco leaves in their peace pipes. On the contrary, almost every tribe had a favorite plant—the yucca, the cattail, and the century plant, among others—whose leaves provided the strong fibers from which Indians wove many of the necessities of life, such as ropes, belts, mats, sandals, baskets, even cloth.

Many tribes were skilled in the use of materials extracted from leaves. For example, there were tribes that used the waxy resins which cover the upper surfaces of so many leaves to waterproof woven baskets and other containers. Northern tribes collected yellow wax from the cigar-shaped leaf buds of the balsam poplar and used it to seal the seams of their birchbark canoes. Most astonishing, though, was a method for preserving food used by Western tribes that roamed through regions where the creosote bush flourishes. How the discovery was made no one knows, but somehow they discovered that a juice drawn from creosote leaves would keep their fatty foods from turning rancid for days on end, even in hot weather!

With the coming of the white man, leaves were sometimes employed in even stranger ways. The records reveal, for instance, that Spanish explorers actually used the large, tough leaves of the coca plums and sea grapes that line Florida's beaches for, of all things, writing paper! Later, other explorers were thankful when they discovered that a weed they knew in Europe also grew in the New World. The leaves of this weed, prickly lettuce, always line up with the path of the sun, half of them pointing east, half west. Thus on dark sunless days, explorers pushing through the wilderness with no compass to guide them could often get their bearings from nature's compass plant.

When the Boston Tea Party brought shipments of tea from England to a halt, our forefathers were abruptly cut off from one of their favorite drinks. Then a company of New Jersey militia discovered a shrub that still grows in most of the forests along our eastern seaboard. Today, however, it is of interest only because of its weird triangular fruit, which when ripe explodes and shoots its seeds off in three directions. But during the Revolution the shrub was eagerly sought for its leaves, which made an excellent substitute for tea and earned for the plant the name it is still known by, New Jersey Tea.

Later in our history, homesteaders in the West used hay and prairie grass to pave muddy wagon trails and to build roads across stretches of loose sand. Twisted into tight bundles, the same leaves also provided homesteaders on treeless plains with fuel for their stoves. And to those pioneers who lived where both the rattlesnake and the yucca, or Spanish bayonet, were common, the long needles on the ends of the yucca leaves were a godsend. Because a man who was bitten by a rattlesnake could save his life by quickly jabbing a yucca needle into the fang wounds and twisting it. This caused heavy bleeding, and as the blood poured from the wound it carried most of the snake's venom with it.

It may seem to you that man in his time has made the oddest possible use of leaves. Yet if we look at some of the things insects do with leaves, we'll find oddities that make man's seem trifling by comparison. For as you may know, the life cycles of certain insects are so closely bound to leaves that the two are inseparable. And the ties that link them together are frequently as fascinating and occasionally as puzzling as anything in nature.

A simple example of a puzzling link between a leaf and an insect can be seen along the shores of the Great Lakes, where the black-and-yellow flower fly lives. This fly, which resembles a honeybee, spends its time like other flies, searching for food by day and sleeping at night. But, astonishingly, it can only sleep on the leaves of one plant, the cinquefoil. What's more, when these flower flies settle down for the night, every one of them goes to sleep in exactly the same position—facing in along a cinquefoil leaf, head close to the stalk, all six feet gripping the leaf's midrib! Why? No one has the slightest idea.

We know why female butterflies stamp about on leaves with their front feet when they are ready to lay their eggs. Through their highly sensitive feet they can feel the difference in texture between one leaf and another. And each female is searching for the right species of plant on which to lay her eggs, so that when her caterpillars hatch out they will have the correct leaves to munch on. But just why one species of caterpillar can digest only one type of leaf, and not others, is still not fully understood.

Much more puzzling is the case of the Mexican acacia shrub. It has two large, curved, hollow spines at the base of each leaf— hence the shrub's name, bull-horn acacia—in which a particular species of ant lives. In addition, the acacia's leaflets have small tooth-shaped tips which are of absolutely no use to the plant because they perform no photosynthetic function. But the "teeth" do provide the ants that live in the bull-horns with their favorite food. Thus the acacia offers its guests both room and board.

The advantages the ants gain from this insect-leaf link is obvious. But how does the acacia profit from the relationship? Here we come to an argument that has gone on for more than a century. One school of botanists insists that the ants living in the bull-horns "possess fiery stings, and are fleet of foot, nervous and belligerent," and that when browsing cattle or leaf-eating ants attack the acacia, its guest ants drive the attackers off with their fiery stings. To this, an opposing school of botanists replies, "Nonsense." These skeptics believe that the sharp bull-horn spines are enough in themselves to discourage grazing cattle. As for leaf-eating ants, they say eyewitnesses have seen the acacia's boarders flee for cover in the face of an invasion by their leaf-hungry cousins.

Confused by the debate, one naturalist says, "It is difficult to arrive at a real evaluation of the ant's role in the whole defensive setup"—which is certainly a safe if not very enlightening comment.

Using leaves either for housing or as a housing material is a common practice in the insect world. Indeed, in the first stage of their lives, hundreds of insects actually house themselves in the almost nonexistent space between the upper and lower surfaces of a leaf. Called leaf miners, they are in most cases the larvae of certain beetles, flies, wasps, and moths that lay their eggs on leaves. (Larvae are immature insects that hatch from eggs in one form and later attain their adult form by a process called metamorphosis. Caterpillars are larvae that wrap themselves in cocoons, go through a stage of metamorphosis, then emerge either as moths or as butterflies.)

Because of the cramped quarters in which they live, leaf miners are, of course, microscopically small. Even so, they all have unusual heads—some wedge-shaped, some with shovel-like jaws—which are especially well suited for burrowing through the interior of a leaf. What is particularly remarkable about leaf miners, though, is that as they bore through leaves, eating their way to freedom, the tunnel each species makes forms its own distinctive pattern. Some are serpentine, some square, some looping, and they are all so individual that experts can tell what species of miner is living unseen within a leaf simply by studying its tunnel pattern. "Leaf miners," it has been said, "write their signatures in leaves."

Some two thousand different insects house their larvae in mysterious structures called galls. Galls can be produced by any part of a plant, but a large percentage of them appear only on leaves. The most common gall is the large brown blister, or ball, sometimes measuring more than an inch in diameter, which you so often see on oak leaves. And what is amazing about the oak leaf and other galls is this—a gall is a nursery for an insect's larvae that is built by a leaf, not an insect!

An oak-leaf gall is a typical example of how galls are produced by leaves in answer to a chemical stimulus provided by an insect. It begins with a gall wasp laying an egg on an oak leaf. When the egg hatches, the wasp's larva injects an as yet unidentified growth substance into the leaf. This unknown chemical "excites," overstimulates, does something to the leaf's cells, and they immediately begin to build a protective tissue over the helpless larva. Even more amazing, the cells coat the inner surface of the structure with a spongy material that provides the larva with food. And to make sure that the gall and the infant it shelters won't be eaten or damaged by other creatures, the oak leaf coats the outer surface of the gall with a bitter-tasting substance, and in addition sometimes fortifies the exterior with sharp hairs or spines!

Since each species of gall insect provokes a leaf into building a gall of a different size or shape, it is the blind guess of botanists that each species secretes a different type of growth substance. To add to the confusion surrounding galls, some larvae when fully grown can tunnel out of their shelters. In other galls, however, the walls are too hard for the larvae to break through.

When this is the case, a leaf may equip its gall with a plug that somehow manages to fall out at the proper time, setting the larva free. Or a leaf may build a timing mechanism into a gall that splits it open at the very moment the larva is ready to emerge. Is it any wonder that scientists shake their heads in awe and puzzlement over galls? Why . . . how . . . what makes leaves labor to produce such extraordinary nurseries for creatures from another world?

Another group of insects takes a more direct approach to building leaf houses. It consists of creatures that spin silken thread, similar to the thread spiders spin to build webs, which they then use to "sew" a leaf, or leaves, together to form nests. One member of the group is the American leaf-rolling cricket. A nighttime eater of smaller insects, at dawn the cricket hides from predatory birds by rolling itself up in a leaf. To do this, the cricket pulls a leaf around its body with its feet, then fastens the leaf's edges together with a silk thread made by special glands in its mouth. Similar nests are built by a family of leaf-rolling caterpillars. And there are bagworm moths that nest in "bags" of evergreen needles woven together with silken threads.

But of all of the creatures that build nests from leaves, none is as skilled as the tree ant of the Indo-Pacific. While ants of this species may in the end use several leaves, they usually begin constructing a nest with a single leaf. Yet folding over even one leaf such as a scrub mahogany—measuring eight by three inches—is a formidable task for ants whose average length is about three-eighths of an inch. Moreover, folding a leaf to provide a roof and a floor for a nest is only half the job. Once folded, the leaf has to be secured in place.

To accomplish their goal, at least a hundred ants swarm onto the edges of a leaf. Then by gripping each other with their jaws, the ants form a number of living chains, with the outer member of each chain grasping an opposite edge of the leaf. Next, with one united tug the several chains of ants pull the outer half of the leaf back over the inner half.

While the chained ants hold the leaf in position, other ants scurry inside the nest, each carrying an ant larva in its jaws. The larva is held by the middle, with its head free, so its mouth can touch an edge of the leaf. Then the larva is carried from one opposing leaf edge to the other, leaving behind a strong and sticky thread of silk. This process is repeated from side to side along the leaf's edges until a web holds them firmly in place. Then the ants usually turn to nearby leaves, tugging and fastening them to the first leaf in order to enlarge and reinforce their nest. So by the time a colony of tiny tree ants finishes its almost unbelievably skillful construction job, it may have a nest as large as a football.

Among the insects that use leaves not as nests but as sources of building material are a number of wild bees. The leaf-cutter bee, for example, snips pieces out of rose leaves, clasps them to the underside of its body, and flies off with them to a nest it has bored into an old tree trunk. There the bee tailors the pieces of leaf into the shape of a thimble. Each fragment of leaf is cleverly made to overlap the next, then glued into position with a secretion from the bee's mouth, like wallpaper. Other species of bees chew leaves into a pulp, which they then use as a form of plaster to smooth the walls of their nests.

There are leaf-cutting ants too. But theirs is quite a different story. Known as *Atta* ants and found mainly in the American tropics, they live together in colonies numbering as many as 600,000, in long underground caves of their own digging. With colonies of such size, *Attas* on the prowl for leaves can easily strip a tree bare in a day. And they do it with uncommon efficiency. For it is their practice to send thousands of workers aloft to snip a tree's leaves into small pieces and drop them to the ground, where ants in even greater numbers pick them up in their hooked jaws and carry them off to the colony's cave. There, in specially dug chambers about the size of a small watermelon, they spread their leaf fragments out, layer upon layer, to a depth of perhaps three inches.

With their nests already dug, why do *Atta* ants work so hard to obtain a supply of leaves? It is because their lives depend in a sense on leaves. For they are ants whose only food is a fungus that is a close relative of the mushroom, and the fungus grows best on a bed of leaves rotting in dark moist surroundings. So, fantastic though it may seem, *Atta* ants grow and harvest their own food crop. Because no sooner do the leaf-carrying ants lay a bed of leaves in one of the colony's underground chambers than other ants hasten to seed it with bits of fungus from a crop already under cultivation!

Finally, there is a South American caterpillar that has found two uses for leaves, one ordinary, the other extraordinary—to put it mildly. The caterpillar eats leaves, which isn't unusual. But the caterpillar happens to have a body that is the same shade of green as the large jungle leaves it feeds on. And before it begins a meal, it first uses its teeth to scissor out of a leaf three to five silhouettes of itself, which match its size, shape, and color. Then with spun threads it attaches the models to one end of the leaf, to distract the eyes of passing birds. This done, the caterpillar crawls to the opposite end of the leaf, to eat in peace and safety.

If any creature, man or insect, has found a stranger use for a leaf, it's certainly not on record.

9: a leaf unfolds

FOR YOU the first day of January may mark the beginning of a new year, but Nature's new year begins with spring, when buds open, young leaves emerge, and a surge of cholorophyll turns the treetops green. Since this is common knowledge, you may wonder why it's worth mentioning. It is because the chances are that you've never really seen exactly how and when spring arrives, no matter how many springs you've lived through. If you're like most people, you've never noticed the miraculous timing with which bud packages suddenly pop open—even though it takes place before your eyes.

Most of us think of spring leafing not as an overnight phenomenon but as a slow and gradual process that takes place over a matter of weeks. This is true only of spring leafing in general. What surprisingly few people realize, though, is that for plants bearing leaf buds spring *does* arrive overnight, on one specific day.

In your home town, for instance, every oak tree leafs out not only in one day but on precisely the same day. Yet the oaks in one part of town are clearly not aware of what those in another section are doing. Nor do all of them live in exactly the same environment. Some grow sheltered from the wind, others exposed. Some grow wild, others have been carefully pruned and fertilized. Even so, when the day to sprout leaves arrives, they all act as one! What is equally amazing is that every leaf bud on a single oak bursts open on the same day too, despite the fact that the buds on its upper and lower and its inner and outer branches have spent the winter under quite different conditions.

Nor are oaks unusual in this respect. On its appointed spring day every broadleaf tree and bush in your home town will also unfold all of its new leaves simultaneously. Yet when we sow seeds, they don't all sprout at the same time. Some may put out their first leaves days later than others. Why, then, should the miracle of exact timing be found only in buds?

According to Dr. Frits Went, "The precision of timing in the bud break of trees suggests that it is under the control of two mechanisms. Since all of the cherry trees in Washington, D.C., break bud at the same time, there is probably an external signal or influence at work. But since cherries usually bud a month before beeches, say, and since both species vary from year to year by a week or more in the time of their budding, the external signal is probably a very complex one, different for each kind of tree. In some cases we know that the signal is connected with the amount of cold a tree has been subjected to in winter. In others it may also be related to spring temperatures."

To understand the nature of these timing mechanisms, you must first know the kinds of buds they influence. They are called winter buds, because they are produced by one year's leaves, lie dormant, or asleep, over winter, then sprout in the spring to become the following year's leaves. Winter buds, moreover, are manufactured only by the leaves of perennials, which is what plants that continue to grow year after year, such as trees and bushes, are called. So winter buds shouldn't be confused with the buds put out by plants that live by a single season, which are called annuals.

None of the buds formed by annual plants are winter buds. Rather they are floral buds that burst into flower, set seeds, then die, all in the same season. Thus annuals reproduce yearly through seeds alone, whereas winter buds bear the responsibility of renewing life year after year for perennials. (Naturally, the very first leaves of perennials are born of seeds too, because perennials begin life as seedlings. And as you know, the immature plant, or embryo, within a seed consists of one or more tiny leaves, as well as a thread for a beginning root and a minute stem for a trunk or a stalk.)

A perennial's leaves are usually free to begin forming buds by midsummer. By then the plant has stopped putting on the new growth which up to that point has been consuming the output of its food factories. In fact, the hottest weeks of the year are sometimes called a perennial's "harvest time," since it is during this period that a plant begins to store food against the coming winter, and its leaves begin to build the winter buds, which are its sole guarantee of another spring flowering. However, since a plant has no way of "telling" its leaves to start forming buds, nature has had to devise a way of letting them know that the moment has arrived. And whether by coincidence or master plan, nature uses a time signal to set in motion the manufacture of buds which will later open in response to yet another time signal.

For years botanists believed that weather alone controlled the precise and regular rhythms of plant life. But they were uneasy in their belief because they knew that weather itself has no precise rhythm and is, instead, highly unpredictable. Then in 1920 they learned that a plant's rhythmic development is largely controlled not by the weather but by one of the most predictable of all natural events—the cycle of the seasons. More specifically, they discovered that as the seasons slide north and south and the sun rises and sets at a different time each day, the changing relationship of daylight to darkness is the signal which causes plants, in turn, to change their activities.

The phenomenon of a plant's reaction to differing lengths of night and day is called photoperiodism ("light-period response"). And we now know that almost every plant has in it clusters of light-sensitive cells that can somehow measure the exact amount of time the sun spends below the horizon. These cells can be compared to an alarm clock, set to go off at a certain photoperiodic signal and awaken a plant to the need to switch its activities to meet the demands of a new season. And the alarm of just such a living clock, which goes off when midsummer nights grow longer, is what prompts a leaf to begin manufacturing a bud.

If you examine a twig on a broadleaf tree during August you can most easily follow a bud's growth, since of all perennial plants broadleaf trees generally produce the largest buds. Even so, at first you will have to look closely to see the pinhead beginnings of a bud at the base of each of the twig's several leaf stalks. By the end of August, though, the mature buds will be so clearly visible that you can see the tiny yet tough scales in which they are encased. These scales, which overlap rather like fish scales, help protect buds from injury, and insect attack.

Break a mature bud open and you will find inside its scaly armor a green tissue that looks much like any other plant tissue —until you place it under a microscope. Then you will begin to appreciate the wonder of a bud. Because only then can you see that, tiny as it is, it nonetheless contains a miniature twig and several miniature leaves, all neatly tucked inside an envelope filled with glucose for their future nourishment. (Some buds contain miniature flowers, but these are not our immediate concern.)

SECTION OF A SHOOT TIP SHOWING SEVERAL BUDS

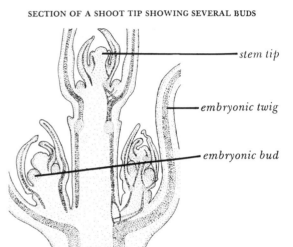

stem tip

embryonic twig

embryonic bud

If you take a microscopic view of a variety of buds, you'll see too that each family of plants has its own way of packaging its embryo leaves. Unborn elm leaves, for example, are folded like fans. Oak leaves are flat but folded face to face along the midrib. Others are rolled inward from both edges; some are rolled like cigars. In all cases, though, the young leaves are folded as carefully as parachutes, so they can interference.

What your microscope won't show, though, are two of a bud's most important features. One is the presence of a speck of wax-like material inside each of the bud's millions of cells—a substance which before frost will change the cells' watery protoplasm into a jelly that doesn't become brittle, like ice, when it freezes. The waxy matter, manufactured and pumped into the cells by the leaf that fathered the bud, protects the protoplasm

91

from injury in zero weather, because once it jells and becomes shatterproof, protoplasm won't break into bits when it is frozen. Thus with the help of an antifreeze mixture a bud's vital supply of protoplasm is kept both alive and intact all winter, ready to go to work as soon as it thaws out.

The second feature of a bud that escapes a microscope's magnifying eye is the mysterious timing mechanism that causes the bud to open in response to a springtime signal.

Here the picture gets a bit cloudy, because botanists are not in full agreement about the nature of the signal that triggers the mechanism. Neither are they sure that the mechanism is keyed to just one signal. Nor are they certain that all perennial plants necessarily respond to the same signal or signals. But despite their differences of opinion, they are inclined to agree that the three most important external factors in control of bud break are photoperiodism, spring warmth, and the amount of cold a bud is subjected to during its winter dormancy.

Most of us can easily understand the role spring warmth might play, because we all know that the ground has to thaw before the sap that swells a bud to the bursting point can begin to flow upward from a plant's roots to its crown. Knowing that plants react to light, we can see too how a photoperiodic signal might play a part in arousing a dormant bud, because as spring creeps northward, each succeeding night grows shorter. But most of us are so accustomed to thinking of cold weather as the sole cause of dormancy that we find it hard to understand how cold can also play a role in awakening a bud from its winter rest.

The surprising fact is that all plants that grow in temperate climates need cold just as much as tropical plants need heat. And if they are perennials, once they go into their winter sleep they simply will not awaken again until after they have experienced a certain amount of cold—as people who mistakenly try to protect young fruit trees by keeping them in a heated greenhouse through the winter soon discover. It is fatal to the trees.

In other words, before a bud can open, it must first live through a winter. This may seem strange, but think of the threat to a bud if it was geared to open to warmth alone. An unseasonably warm period in midwinter could be a false signal that would cause it to open prematurely, only to be killed by frost when cold set in again. So for its own protection, a perennial plant contains a device that is somehow able to measure its regional weather patterns. When its measurements show that a bud has lived through a period of winter cold typical of its local climate, the mechanism in some mysterious way is then able to indicate to a bud that winter has ended. In effect, it tells the bud that it is no longer in danger of being tricked by unseasonable weather and that any rise in temperature it now reacts to will be genuine springtime warmth.

This, at least, is apparently how Dr. Frits Went sees the matter, for according to him, "it takes the double signal of winter's cold and spring's first warmth" to trigger a bud's opening. But he also admits, "Just what the mechanism involved in this quite marvelous phenomenon consists of, we do not know. There may be some chemical inhibitor [a compound that prevents a bud's opening] which is gradually broken down by cold, but if so, it still awaits discovery."

If a chemical inhibitor is involved, it may vary from plant to plant. And if it does vary, this could explain, for example, why a cherry tree leafs out a month ahead of a neighboring birch tree. However, if exactly the same chemical inhibitor is present in all perennials, it may be that once it breaks down and loses its strength, their buds are then timed to open in response to a spring-temperature reading that differs for each individual species, which is what Dr. Went suggests. Or it could be, as some botanists suspect, that different buds react to different photoperiodic signals as the spring nights gradually shorten.

Whatever the case may be, scientists are at least sure of two things. First, that buds do have timing mechanisms which are triggered by one or more external signals. Otherwise there would be no accounting for the fact, say, that an oak tree in Vermont breaks bud several weeks later than an oak in Maryland.

Second, botanists also know that the moment a dormant tree receives its signal it immediately comes to life. At once the sap stored in the tree's roots begins its upward flow through the xylem tubes. As the sap pours into the tree's thousands upon thousands of buds, they begin to swell, and continue swelling until they silently explode—all, miraculously, on the same day. And when they explode, the miniature leaves and twigs the buds have harbored over the winter are instantly thrust forth into the sun.

Thus new leaves are literally born overnight. They are, however, immature leaves that are not yet green with chlorophyll. Rather they are colored one of the shimmering hues that characterize young leaves; ruby red, yellow, crimson, pinkish-golden, even lavender. Nor are the newborn leaves fully unfurled. Instead they are limp and soggy. But they are covered with glistening drops of moisture which act as magnifying lenses. And as these lenses focus the first warm rays of sunlight on their folds, the young leaves start to unfurl, slowly begin to manufacture chlorophyll, and gradually ready themselves in every way for the season of unceasing work that lies ahead.

Over the years much has been written about the wonders of a winter bud. Yet nothing that has been said has shown a deeper understanding of their significance than a few pointed words penned by John Muir, the famed naturalist for whom Alaska's Muir Glacier and California's Muir Woods National Monument were named. After his death, friends found a book of essays he had carried with him as he roamed the wilderness of the Sierra Nevada Mountains in the 1870's. On one page the book's author had made the statement, "Nature ever works and advances, yet takes no thought for the morrow." Muir had underlined the sentence, then written on the margin of the page: "Are not buds and seeds Nature's thought for the morrow?"

10: death of a leaf

EVERY AUTUMN we Americans enjoy an awe-inspiring spectacle never seen by most of the world's people—the blaze of color that sweeps across the landscape as our native leaves go into their scarlet and gold death throes. For the little-known truth is that the glowing colors which flare up each fall in the woodlands of the United States, and particularly in those of the eastern half of the country, are far, far richer and more varied than any found elsewhere in the world.

In the tropics and semitropics, where there are no marked seasonal changes, trees and plants customarily shed their old leaves a few at a time throughout the year. The same is of course true of the evergreens that compose the world's northernmost forests and the treeline forests on high mountains. Indeed, fall foliage displays worthy of the name are seen only in North America, the British Isles, west-central Europe, eastern China, and parts of Japan. Compared to ours, though, the displays seen in other countries are drab and unexciting.

Our autumn scenery surpasses all others for two reasons. For one, the crisp nights and clear sunny days typical of our falls have much to do with the many-colored splendors of the season. In England, China, and Japan, on the other hand, the season is usually mild and cloudy, with the result that their fall foliage is largely limited to dull yellows and browns. Secondly, as a rule foreign forests are composed of only a relatively few deciduous trees, shrubs, vines, and bushes. (Plants that shed their leaves in winter are called deciduous, from the Latin verb *decidere,* meaning "to fall off.") In contrast, our woodlands contains scores of varieties of deciduous plants, each with leaves that contribute their own distinctively vivid hue to the countryside as they end their lives in a blaze of glory.

Think of some of the dazzling colors that make our early fall days beautiful beyond comparison. There is the scarlet of sumac leaves, the lemony yellow of the elms, swamp maple leaves as orange-red as a tanager's wings, and the ruddy bronze of the basswoods' leaves. There are birch, sycamore, and aspen clothed in metallic gold, and deep purple and crimson-sheeted clumps of viburnum. Bluish-pink, orange, crimson, and sunlight-gold intermingle in the leaves of the sugar maple. There is the fiery red of the Virginia creeper, the blue and eggplant purple of the ash. The oaks add touches of ruby and maroon and burgundy, and countless shades of warm, leathery brown. As anyone who looks closely can see, there is in our autumn finery a range of color as wide as it is breathtaking.

For botanists, autumn's numerous colors have raised numerous questions. Yet while it is true that science still hasn't fully deciphered the secret of painted leaves, we do know many of its details. For one thing, research has shown that, contrary to popular belief, frost plays no role in coloring leaves. It is all done by a plant's internal chemistry. And the chemical changes are almost certainly set in motion by one of the photoperiodic signals which, as we have seen, largely control the regular rhythms of plant life.

Broadly speaking, this is what happens. As winter approaches, there comes a point when the changing relationship of daylight to darkness signals a plant that it is time to shut down its leaf factories. They have to be closed before winter sets in because, as you know, transpiring leaves are wasteful of water. And if they aren't shed they will go on wasting water until the ground freezes. So a perennial plant must drop its leaves before the ground hardens, in order to retain a sufficient supply of moisture to keep its cells and tissues alive during the cold months when water is frozen in the soil and no longer available to it.

The process of first shutting down and then shedding their leaf factories is never a problem for a deciduous plant because, amazingly, its leaves began preparing themselves for death at the very moment they were born! If you examine a live deciduous leaf closely you will see at the base of its stalk either a tiny furrow or a narrow circle of tissue of a lighter shade of green than the remainder of the petiole. What you see is called a leaf's separation layer. It is formed when a leaf first sprouts in the spring and enlarges as a leaf increases in size during the growing season. But it takes no active part in a leaf's life until the shortening days of early fall give warning of the coming of winter.

Although it is called *a* separation layer it actually consists of two distinctly different layers of specialized tissues. One layer is made up of cells that start to disintegrate as soon as they receive the autumnal photoperiodic signal. As these cells shrink and weaken, they gradually form a tear-line, like the perforations on a sheet of postage stamps. And once the tear-line is completed, any breeze may blow a leaf off, or it may fall of its own weight.

Below the tear-line tissue is a layer of cells which, instead of weakening, toughen up to form a thin sheet of corklike material. The corky material serves two purposes. It bandages the wound, or scar, left on a twig by a falling leaf and thus protects the twig from attack by insects and bacteria. And it also forms tiny corks to plug the open ends of the xylem and phloem tubes which during the summer extended into the leaf, thereby sealing off the pipelines of the plant's plumbing system. (If you study a twig's horseshoe-shaped leaf scars through a magnifying glass you will see tiny dots that remind one of the nail holes in a horseshoe. The dots are really the little corks in the ends of the xylem and phloem tubes.)

It takes about two weeks for the separation layer to finish its work, and it is during these weeks that autumn puts on its richest display. This is because the slow formation of the corky layer gradually clogs more and more of the pipelines leading into the leaf. And as the leaf begins to receive less and less water from its roots, it grows less and less able to renew the chlorophyll which gives it its intense green color. Nor is the leaf long able to maintain the "green blood" it already holds, because chlorophyll must have fresh water or it disappears. So with no water to sustain it, the old chlorophyll simply wastes away. And as it fades it uncovers two colorful chemical compounds, called pigments, which were hidden in the leaf all summer long.

If you'll recall, in describing bud break we said that when leaves first unfold they are not yet green with chlorophyll, which they have to manufacture, but are instead yellow, crimson, pinkish-golden, lavender, or one of the other shimmering hues characteristic of young leaves. These colors are the product of two pigments, carotene and xanthophyll, which are present in leaves from the beginning. Why they are present, no one really knows, though some scientists think they may be chemical compounds which in some way help chlorophyll manufacture glucose.

Whatever their purpose, we know that carotene and xanthophyll are pigments capable of producing a surprising variety of colors, ranging from yellow to mahogany and from crimson to orange. We know too that they are among the commonest pigments in nature. In addition to painting autumn leaves, they furnish the color we find in egg yolks, ears of corn, carrots, orange zinnias, the feathers of a canary, and many other natural objects. But whereas their colors aren't ordinarily hidden, in a leaf their hue is masked throughout the summer by a heavy blanket of chlorophyll green and doesn't reappear until the chlorophyll bleaches out of a leaf in the fall.

Carotene and xanthophyll do not account, however, for the most brilliant colors of autumn—the flaming reds and deep purples. These are formed by a group of pigments known as anthocyanins, also common throughout the plant kingdom. For example, red apples, cranberries, poppies, purple grapes, violets, radishes, and poinsettias all get their colors from anthocyanins.

The vivid colors of the anthocyanins are never seen in a leaf, though, before the separation layer has begun to close down its operation. This is because anthocyanins are a late development in a leaf, the product of a chemical reaction that takes place once the sun's rays focus their energy on the glucose that is trapped in a leaf *after* its food-distributing phloem tubes have been plugged up. For when the corky layer seals off a leaf, there is always some glucose left in it, as well as some chlorophyll, which will, before it decomposes, manufacture still more glucose. And the more glucose a sealed-up leaf holds, the brighter and more intense the color that results—*if* the sun has the time and the strength to fully convert the glucose into anthocyanins.

The "if" in part explains why fall colors vary in brightness from year to year. Because for the season to look its finest, the anthocyanins must form quickly and fully. And we know that they develop best when they are exposed to strong and steady sunlight. In experiments, letters cut out of adhesive tape have been stuck on leaves just before they were ready to turn. When the letters were later removed, words were found dimly printed on the leaves. The portions of the leaves shielded from the sun had not produced anthocyanins.

Thus for our woodlands to reach their greatest beauty, we know we must have a series of bright, sunny autumn days. But for reasons not clearly understood, we know too that other weather factors are also involved. For one, the record shows that an ideal foliage display calls first for a fairly dry period in late summer. Then, when the sunny days of early autumn arrive, they must be accompanied by a series of crisp, cool nights, with temperatures around the low forties. It follows, obviously, that an autumn of cloudy days and mild nights produces the least brilliant colors. And if a hard frost comes too early in the season, it can turn leaves a drab brown almost overnight. (Knowing this, you should be able to predict how colorful the leaves will be in your area next fall.)

Strangely enough, autumn colors apparently play no practical role whatsoever in nature's scheme of things. This is both surprising and puzzling, since nature seldom wastes energy to no purpose. Yet insofar as botanists can determine, the chemical energy that goes into the painting of a leaf is of no benefit at all to a plant. The colors seem merely to herald the end of a leaf's life cycle.

But while the dazzling splendor of a leaf's slow death seems to serve no purpose, in death itself a leaf's usefulness is by no means ended. For when dead leaves flutter to the ground—as many as ten million to a single acre of woodland—they carry with them an immense and precious cargo of left-over mineral salts; a treasury of sulfur, calcium, iron, potassium, phosphorus, magnesium, and every other element essential to life. Then, lying at the very feet of the plants that bore them, they in time decay and release their treasure to the soil. Later, spring rains carry the vital elements to awakening roots. And there they are absorbed and carried skyward to nourish a new crop of leaves and ensure another year of healthy growth.

Thus the story of leaves is in essence the story of all life. For when their time is up, all living things must die and give way to new generations which they helped create. In this sense, then, life is immortal, because the basic elements of life—the stuff of which the living protoplasm of the cell is made—survives, to return to the soil and sustain new life. The soil then gives life to plants and leaves. With their leaves' help, plants in turn provide food for animals. And they in their turn sustain other creatures, ourselves included. Thus life cycle flows into life cycle in a never-ending round. Thus too, a leaf that has fallen in death returns its borrowed substance to the soil, so that generations of plants and men as yet unborn will never lack for nourishment.

Knowing this, you can see why the great nineteenth-century Russian writer Fyodor Dostoevski urged all of us to, "Love every leaf, every ray of God's light. Love the plants, love the animals, love everything. If you love everything you will sense the divine mystery in things. Once you sense it, you will begin to understand it better every day. And you will come at last to love the whole world."

bibliography

Asimov, Isaac, *The Intelligent Man's Guide to Science*. New York, Basic Books, Inc., 1960.

Barrow, George, *Your World in Motion*. New York, Harcourt, Brace & World, Inc., 1956.

Coulter, Merle C., and Howard J. Dittmer, *The Story of the Plant Kingdom*. Chicago, The University of Chicago Press, 1964.

Dawson, E. Yale, *Marine Botany*. New York, Holt, Rinehart and Winston, Inc., 1966.

Farb, Peter, *The Forest*. New York, Life Nature Library, 1961.

Farmer, J. Bretland, *Plant Life*. New York, Henry Holt & Co., 1913.

Fogg, G. E., *The Growth of Plants*. Baltimore, Md., Penguin Books, 1963.

Galston, Arthur W., *The Life of the Green Plant*. Englewood Cliffs, N.J., Prentice-Hall, Inc., 1964.

Hotchkiss, Neil, *Underwater and Floating-Leaved Plants of the United States and Canada*. Washington, D.C., U.S. Department of the Interior, Bureau of Sport Fisheries and Wildlife, 1967.

Hutchins, Ross E., *Insects*. Englewood Cliffs, N.J., Prentice-Hall, Inc., 1966.

——, *This Is a Leaf*. New York, Dodd, Mead & Company, 1962.

Johnson, Willis H., and William C. Sture, eds., *This Is Life*. New York, Holt, Rinehart and Winston, Inc., 1962.

Kroeber, Elsbeth, Richard L. Weaver, and Walter H. Wolff, *Biology.* Boston, D. C. Heath and Company, 1965.

Leopold, A. Starker, *The Desert.* New York, Life Nature Library, 1961.

Mavor, James Watt, *General Biology.* New York, The Macmillan Co., 1958.

Milne, Lorus J. and Margery, *The Mountains.* New York, Life Nature Library, 1962.

———, *Patterns of Survival.* Englewood Cliffs, N.J., Prentice-Hall, Inc., 1967.

Moore, Alma Chesnut, *The Grasses.* New York, The Macmillan Co., 1960.

Peattie, Donald Culross, *Flowering Earth.* New York, The Viking Press, 1961.

Platt, Rutherford, *The Great American Forest.* Englewood Cliffs, N.J., Prentice-Hall, Inc., 1965.

Pond, Alonzo W., *Deserts: Silent Lands of the World.* New York, W. W. Norton & Co., Inc., 1965.

Ray, Peter Martin, *The Living Plant.* New York, Holt, Rinehart and Winston, Inc., 1966.

Stefferud, Alfred, ed., *Trees.* Washington, D.C., U.S. Department of Agriculture, 1949.

Storer, John H., *The Web of Life.* New York, The Devin-Adair Company, 1954.

Teale, Edwin Way, *Autumn Across America.* New York, Dodd, Mead & Co., 1956.

———, Ed., *Green Treasury.* New York, Dodd, Mead & Co., 1952.

———, *Journey into Summer.* New York, Dodd, Mead & Co., 1960.

———, *Journey into Winter.* New York, Dodd, Mead & Co., 1966.

———, *North with Spring.* New York, Dodd, Mead & Co., 1951.

Thomson, J. Arthur, *Biology for Everyman.* New York, E. P. Dutton & Co., Inc., 1935.

———, *The Outline of Science.* New York, Putnam's, 1922.

Waltereck, Heinz, *The Miracle of Life.* London, Souvenir Press Ltd., 1963.

Went, Frits W., *The Plants.* New York, Life Nature Library, 1963.

Wideman, Charles J., and Raphaelis Gehlen, *The Biological World.* Chicago, Loyola University Press, 1962.

Wrightman, William P. D., *The Growth of Scientific Ideas.* New Haven, Conn., Yale University Press, 1953.

———, *The Harper Encyclopedia of Science* (4 vols.), ed. by James R. Newman. New York, Harper & Row, Inc., 1963.

Bibliography

——, *The Illustrated Library of the Natural Sciences,* sponsored by the American Museum of Natural History. New York, Simon and Schuster, 1958.

——, *Plant Life,* a Scientific American Book. New York, Simon and Schuster, 1957.

index

Index

rainfall
  desert, 48
  plants' relation to, 32–33
root growth, rate of, 33–34, 63
root pressure, 35
roots
  and leaves, cooperation between, 33
  glucose supply for, 14
  needles as substitutes for, 46

Saussure, Nicolas Theodore de,
    glucose analysis by, 9–10
sensitive plant, 73–74
separation layer, function of, 98–99
sleep movements, 74
soil, as source of plant food, 4, 5
Spanish moss, 52–53, 56
sponge cells, function of, 23
spring leafing, 87–88
spring warmth, bud opening related
    to, 92, 93
stalk, of a leaf, 13
  function of, 14
stem tips, growth substance secreted
    by, 64–66, 69
stomata
  aquatic plants', 41
  function of, 24–25, 35, 36, 39, 40, 63
  Welwitschia trees', 48
sugars, composition of, 9
sundew plants 60–61
sunlight, 6, 14, 26
  effect of, on leaves, 9, 22–23
sun's energy, 26
survival, adaptability essential to, 43–
    45

tear-line, 99
telegraph plant, 75
tendrils, 51
  effect of thigmotropism on, 73
thigmotropism, 73
Thomson, Sir J. Arthur
  cell's role explained by, 19
  comment by, on telegraph plant, 75
thorns, 54
time signals, bud-opening, 89, 94
timing mechanisms, budding influ-
    enced by, 88–89, 92, 94
tissues, 15–16
transpiration, plants', 29–40
  definition of, 30
  process of, reversed, 46, 50
tree, comparison of, to city, 19
tree-dwelling plants, 53, 56
turgor, 38–39, 67
turgor movement, 74

Van Helmont, Jan Baptista, experi-
    ment by, a challenge to
    Aristotle's theory, 4–5
vascular bundles, 13
veins, of a leaf, 13, 14
Venus's-flytrap, 61–62

water
  distribution of, in plant, 13
  forms of, 32
  importance of, to life, 18
  leaves supply of, 23–24
  nature of, 36
  as plant-food source, 4–5, 6, 9
  plants' search for, 33–34